First World War
and Army of Occupation
War Diary
France, Belgium and Germany

58 DIVISION
Divisional Troops
Machine Gun Corps
58 Battalion
2 March 1918 - 31 May 1919

WO95/2996/11

The Naval & Military Press Ltd
www.nmarchive.com
Published in association with The National Archives

Published by

The Naval & Military Press Ltd

Unit 10 Ridgewood Industrial Park,

Uckfield, East Sussex,

TN22 5QE England

Tel: +44 (0) 1825 749494

www.naval-military-press.com

www.nmarchive.com

This diary has been reprinted in facsimile from the original. Any imperfections are inevitably reproduced and the quality may fall short of modern type and cartographic standards.

Contents

Document type	Place/Title	Date From	Date To
Heading	WO95/2996/11		
Heading	58 Div 58 Bn Machine Gun Corps 1916 Mar-1919 Apl		
War Diary	Chauny	02/03/1918	02/03/1918
War Diary	Divisional Sector Astride River Oise	02/03/1918	18/03/1918
War Diary	Quierzy	19/03/1918	31/03/1918
War Diary	58th Divisional Sector Astride River Oise	20/00/1918	24/00/1918
Miscellaneous	To D.A.G 3rd Echelon		
War Diary	Yaucourt Busses	01/05/1918	05/05/1918
War Diary	Mirvaux	06/05/1918	07/05/1918
War Diary	Molliens Au Bois	08/05/1918	16/05/1918
War Diary	Contay	17/05/1918	31/05/1918
Miscellaneous	Move Orders		
Operation(al) Order(s)	Operation Orders No.7 By Lieut Col. P.D. Stewart. D.S.O. Commanding 58th Battalion Machine Gun Corps	14/05/1918	14/05/1918
Operation(al) Order(s)	Operation Orders No.8 By Lieut Col. P.D. Stewart. D.S.O. Commanding 58th Battalion Machine Gun Corps	15/05/1918	15/05/1918
Operation(al) Order(s)	Operation Orders No.9 By Lieut Col. P.D. Stewart. D.S.O. Commanding 58th Battalion Machine Gun Corps	18/05/1918	18/05/1918
Miscellaneous	Amendment To Operation Order No. 9	19/05/1918	19/05/1918
Operation(al) Order(s)	Order No. 10 By Lieut Col P.D. Stewart D.S.O. Commanding 58th Battalion Machine Gun Corps		
Operation(al) Order(s)	Order No. 11 By Lieut Col P.D. Stewart D.S.O. Commanding 58th Battalion Machine Gun Corps	24/05/1918	24/05/1918
Miscellaneous	D.A.G. 3rd Echelon	01/07/1918	01/07/1918
War Diary	Contay	01/06/1918	01/06/1918
War Diary	Mirvaux	02/06/1918	10/06/1918
War Diary	Fourdrinoy	11/06/1918	17/06/1918
War Diary	Molliens Aux Bois Wood	18/06/1918	18/06/1918
War Diary	Molliens And Bois	18/06/1918	18/06/1918
War Diary	Ebarts Farm	19/06/1918	30/06/1918
Operation(al) Order(s)	58th Battalion Machine Gun Corps Order No. 12	31/05/1918	31/05/1918
Miscellaneous	Relief Table for 58th Battalion Machine Gun Corps Order no. 12		
Operation(al) Order(s)	58th Battalion Machine Gun Corps Order No. 13	16/06/1918	16/06/1918
Operation(al) Order(s)	58th Battalion Machine Gun Corps Order No. 14	26/06/1918	26/06/1918
War Diary	Ebarts Farm	01/07/1918	31/07/1918
Operation(al) Order(s)	58th Battalion Machine Gun Corps Order No. 16	16/07/1918	16/07/1918
Miscellaneous	Amendment To Order No. 16	23/07/1918	23/07/1918
Operation(al) Order(s)	58th Battalion Machine Gun Corps Special Order	20/07/1918	20/07/1918
Operation(al) Order(s)	58th Battalion Machine Gun Corps Order No. 17	24/07/1918	24/07/1918
Operation(al) Order(s)	58th Battalion Machine Gun Corps Order No. 19	26/07/1918	26/07/1918
Operation(al) Order(s)	58th Battalion Machine Gun Corps Order No. 18	25/07/1918	25/07/1918
Operation(al) Order(s)	58th Battalion Machine Gun Corps Order No. 20	28/07/1918	28/07/1918
Operation(al) Order(s)	58th Battalion Machine Gun Corps Order No. 21	29/07/1918	29/07/1918
Operation(al) Order(s)	58th Battalion Machine Gun Corps Order No. 22	31/07/1918	31/07/1918
Heading	War Diary 58th Battalion Machine Gun Corps April 1918		

War Diary	Blerancourt	01/04/1918	04/04/1918
War Diary	Glisy	05/04/1918	14/04/1918
War Diary	Fort Manoir Farm	15/04/1918	19/04/1918
War Diary	Glisy	20/04/1918	28/04/1918
War Diary	Yaucourt Bussus	29/04/1918	30/04/1918
Heading	58th Divl. Troops 58th Battalion Machine Gun Corps August 1918		
War Diary	Ebarts Farm	01/08/1918	04/08/1918
War Diary	Pont Noyelles	04/08/1918	16/08/1918
War Diary	Key Wood	17/08/1918	22/08/1918
Miscellaneous	Operations Of The 58th Division From 8-13 August 1918 Machine Guns	15/08/1918	15/08/1918
Diagram etc	Diagram		
Miscellaneous	Forthcoming Operations 58th (London) Divisional Instructions No.4	05/08/1918	05/08/1918
Operation(al) Order(s)	58th Battalion Machine Gun Corps Order No. 23	01/08/1918	01/08/1918
Miscellaneous	Addendum No.1 To Order No. 24	06/08/1918	06/08/1918
Operation(al) Order(s)	58th Battalion Machine Gun Corps Order No. 24	06/08/1918	06/08/1918
Miscellaneous	58th (London) Divisional Instructions No.4	05/08/1918	05/08/1918
Miscellaneous	Operations Of The 58th Division From 8-13 August 1918 Machine Guns	15/08/1918	15/08/1918
Operation(al) Order(s)	58th Battalion, Machine Gun Corps Order No. 25	21/08/1918	21/08/1918
Miscellaneous	Narrative Of Events		
Miscellaneous	58 Div. "A"	09/09/1918	09/09/1918
War Diary	A19 F N' Carnoy	01/09/1918	01/09/1918
War Diary	B19 Central	02/09/1918	25/09/1918
War Diary	Caterpillar Wood	26/09/1918	26/09/1918
War Diary	Grand Servins	27/09/1918	28/09/1918
War Diary	Fosse 2	29/09/1918	30/09/1918
Miscellaneous	Appendix 1 Narrative of Events from September 6-25 58th Battalion Machine Gun Corps		
Miscellaneous	Appendix A 58th Battalion Machine Gun Corps.	09/09/1918	09/09/1918
Miscellaneous	58th Battalion Machine Gun Corps	12/09/1918	12/09/1918
Operation(al) Order(s)	58th Battalion Machine Gun Corps Operation Order No. 32	15/09/1918	15/09/1918
Miscellaneous	58th Battalion Machine Gun Corps	16/09/1918	16/09/1918
Operation(al) Order(s)	58th Battalion Machine Gun Corps Operation Order No. 33		
Map	Map		
Operation(al) Order(s)	58th Battalion Machine Gun Corps Operation Order No. 34	19/09/1918	19/09/1918
Operation(al) Order(s)	58th Battalion Machine Gun Corps Operation Order No. 35	20/09/1918	20/09/1918
Diagram etc	Diagram		
Operation(al) Order(s)	58th Battalion Machine Gun Corps Operation Order No. 36	20/09/1918	20/09/1918
Operation(al) Order(s)	58th Battalion Machine Gun Corps Order No. 37	25/09/1918	25/09/1918
Operation(al) Order(s)	58th Battalion Machine Gun Corps Operation Order No. 58	28/09/1918	28/09/1918
Miscellaneous	Embussing Programme		
Miscellaneous	58 Division "A"	07/11/1918	07/11/1918
War Diary	Fosse 2. L 28C	01/10/1918	02/10/1918
War Diary	Fosse 2	02/10/1918	12/10/1918
War Diary	Maroc	13/10/1918	16/10/1918
War Diary	Montigny O23a 2550	16/10/1918	19/10/1918
War Diary	Bersee	19/10/1918	20/10/1918

War Diary	Planard	21/10/1918	29/10/1918
War Diary	Planard B 30 C	29/10/1918	31/10/1918
Operation(al) Order(s)	58th Battalion Machine Gun Corps Order No. 39	07/10/1918	07/10/1918
Operation(al) Order(s)	58th Battalion Machine Gun Corps Order No. 40	14/10/1918	14/10/1918
Miscellaneous	58th Battalion Machine Gun Corps Warning Order	15/10/1918	15/10/1918
Miscellaneous	58th Battalion Machine Gun Corps	19/10/1918	19/10/1918
Miscellaneous	58th Battalion Machine Gun Corps	20/10/1918	20/10/1918
Miscellaneous	Appendix 5th Bn MGC		
Map	Map		
War Diary	Planard B.30.c	01/11/1918	08/11/1918
War Diary	Bleharies D.19.d.6.4	09/11/1918	09/11/1918
War Diary	Wiers E.5.a.05.25	10/11/1918	10/11/1918
War Diary	Beloeil B.3.c.8.3	11/11/1918	18/11/1918
War Diary	Roucourt F.14.d.70.25	19/11/1918	30/11/1918
Miscellaneous	Instructions For Forthcoming Operations	07/11/1918	07/11/1918
Map	Map		
War Diary	Roucourt F.14.d.70.25	01/12/1918	31/12/1918
War Diary	Roucourt F.14.d.72	01/01/1919	31/01/1919
Miscellaneous	58th Division "A"	01/03/1919	01/03/1919
War Diary	Roucourt	01/02/1919	23/02/1919
War Diary	Leuze	24/02/1919	28/02/1919
War Diary	Leuze (Belgium)	01/03/1919	31/03/1919
Miscellaneous	H.Qrs 58th Divl. Group	30/04/1919	30/04/1919
War Diary	Leuze (Belgium)	01/04/1919	31/05/1919

58 DIV

58 DIV MACHINE GUN CORPS.

1918 MAR — 1919 APL

Page 1.

Instructions regarding War Diaries and Intelligence Summaries are contained in F. S. Regs., Part II. and the Staff Manual respectively. Title pages will be prepared in manuscript.

WAR DIARY
or
~~INTELLIGENCE SUMMARY.~~
(Erase heading not required.)

58th Battn Machine Gun Corps

From March 1st to 31st 1918.

Army Form C. 2118.

Place	Date	Hour	Summary of Events and Information	Remarks and references to Appendices
CHAUNY.	2nd		Formation of 58th Battalion M.G. Corps – Headquarters assembled at CHAUNY.	Ref. Maps.
			Commanding Officer – Capt (A/Lt. Col.) P.D. STEWART, D.S.O. – 3rd DRAGOON GUARDS (not present at formation)	66C.
			2nd in Command – Capt (T/Major) M.W. TAIT, M.C. 14th COUNTY OF LONDON REGIMENT (LONDON SCOTTISH). Seconded M.G. CORPS.	66D. 70.D. 70 E } 1/40000
			Adjutant. – Lieut. C.B. FELTON – 215 Co. Machine Gun Corps.	
			Transport Officer – 2nd Lieut R.C. HALL – 215 Co. Machine Gun Corps.	
			Personnel of Battalion H.Q. (with a few exceptions) were drawn from within the Four Machine Gun Companies in the Division	
			Personnel to complete the increased establishment of Companies drawn from Infantry Battalions within the Division.	
			Transport. – drawn from within the Division – previously belonging to the disbanded Battalions.	
			Designations of M.G. Companies	

Old Title	New Title	Officer Commanding Company		
206. Coy.	"A" Coy	Capt.	C.J.C. Pullar.	1st Seaforths and M.G.C.
198 Coy.	"B" Coy	Capt	J.S. Palliser	5th Yorks and M.G.C.
215 Coy.	"C" Coy	Capt	H.D. Drew.	M.G. Corps.
214 Coy.	"D" Coy.	Capt	C.J. Morris.	M.G. Corps

D. D. & L., London, E.C.
(A8004) Wt. W1771/M2-31 750,000 5/17 Sch 52 Forms/C2118/14

58

Army Form C. 2118.

WAR DIARY
or
~~INTELLIGENCE SUMMARY.~~
(Erase heading not required.)

Instructions regarding War Diaries and Intelligence Summaries are contained in F. S. Regs., Part II. and the Staff Manual respectively. Title pages will be prepared in manuscript.

Place	Date	Hour	Summary of Events and Information	Remarks and references to Appendices
Divisional Sector astride River OISE.	2nd		DISPOSITIONS. 58th (London) Division holding the Line from about 2000x S. of VENDEUIL on the North to CARRIERES BERNAGOUSSE (about 1000x S of BARISIS) a frontage of about 15000 yards. Machine Gun Companies holding the Line with Brigades as follows:- LEFT SECTOR. from N. Boundary to RIVER OISE – 173 Infantry Brigade – "A" M.G. Coy. CENTRE SECTOR. from RIVER OISE to POPLAR PLANTATION – 175 Infantry Brigade – "C" M.G. Coy. RIGHT SECTOR. 174 Infantry Brigade – "B" M.G. Coy. RESERVE. "D" M.G. Coy in Divisional Reserve. 18th DIVISION on the Left .... FRENCH ARMY on the Right.	Ref. Maps. 66C. 66D. } 1/40000 70D. 70E.

	Headquarters.	Transport Lines
Divisional H.Q.	QUIERZY	
M.G. Bn. H.Q.	CHAUNY	CHAUNY.
"A" Coy.	QUESSY.	VIRY NOUREUIL
"B" Coy	CARRIERES BERNAGOUSSE	MARIZELLE.
"C" Coy	BUTTES de ROUY.	....
"D" Coy	MARIZELLE.	....

DISPOSITIONS OF SECTIONS.

	Forward Zone	Battle Zone.	Reserve.
A.	1 Section + 1 Gun.	3 Sections less 1 Gun.	1. Section "D" Coy.
B	2 Sections	2. Sections	1 Section "D" Coy.
C	1 Section + 1 Gun.	3 Sections less 1 Gun	1 Section "D" Coy.
D	3 Sections attached to A, B, C. Coys (1 each)	1. Section in Div. Reserve in MARIZELLE.	

} Sections of "D" Co. were interchangeable with the Sections of the Companies to which they were attached.

[signature]

D. D. & L., London, E.C.
(A8004) Wt. W1771/M2031 750,000 5/17 Sch. 52 Forms/C2118/14

Instructions regarding War Diaries and Intelligence Summaries are contained in F. S. Regs., Part II. and the Staff Manual respectively. Title pages will be prepared in manuscript.

WAR DIARY
or
~~INTELLIGENCE SUMMARY.~~
(Erase heading not required.)

Army Form C. 2118.

Place	Date	Hour	Summary of Events and Information	Remarks and references to Appendices
	3rd, 4th, 5th, 6th, 7th, 8th, 9th		Machine Gun Battalion H.Q in course of formation and organisation.	Ref. Maps. 66C., 66D., 70D., 70E. 1/40000.
	10th		Lieut D.S. LINDSAY (2nd in Command "D" Coy) to 63rd Bn. M.G. Corps.	
	11th		Lieut and Q.M. G.M. WILLIAMS - Rifle Brigade arrived and assumed duties as Battalion Quartermaster.	
	12th		Advanced Coy H.Q of "B" Company in CARRIERES BERNAGOUSSE destroyed by big explosion of French ammunition in close proximity.	
			Casualties - "B" Coy. - 2 Other Ranks Missing. "D" Coy - 1 Other Rank Missing. 2 Other Ranks Wounded.	
			(Bodies of the 3 Missing men recovered by digging on 16th).	
	13th			
	14th		Lieut A.P.S. BORTHWICK arrived from Base - posted to "D" Company.	
			Lieut L. KAVANAUGH., U.S.R., M.C. arrived and assumed duties as Battalion Medical Officer.	
	15th		Capt R.J. REID - to U.K.	
	16th			
	17th			
	18th		Battalion H.Q moved from CHAUNY to QUIERZY.	
QUIERZY.	19th		LIEUT. COL. P.D. STEWART arrived and assumed command of the Battalion from the 20th inst.	
	20th		All men resting, in anticipation of enemy attack on 21st inst.	
			1. Gun of "A" Company placed at CONDREN to cover Marsh E. of that village.	
			Lieut J.R. ROBSON arrived from Base Depot and evacuated sick same day.	[initials]

D. D. & L., London, E.C.
(A8004) Wt. W1771/M2131 750,000 5/17 Sch. 52 Forms/C2118/14

Instructions regarding War Diaries and Intelligence Summaries are contained in F. S. Regs., Part II. and the Staff Manual respectively. Title pages will be prepared in manuscript.

WAR DIARY
or
~~INTELLIGENCE SUMMARY~~.
(Erase heading not required.)

Army Form C. 2118.

Place	Date	Hour	Summary of Events and Information	Remarks and references to Appendices
X.	21st		Commencement of Enemy offensive.	
X.	22nd }		"A" and "D" Companies in action	
X.	23rd }		with 173rd Infantry Brigade.	
	23rd	12 noon	"A" Company moved from OGNES to APPILLY	
			"D" Company Transport and spare men to APPILLY.	
	24th		Battalion H.Q. from QUIERZY to BESME.	
			"A" Company from APPILLY to BESME.	
			"D" " " " " "	
			"B" and "C" Companies' Transport moved from MARIZELLE to BAC D'ARBLINCOURT (attacked by enemy aeroplane whilst on the road.) 2 horses killed.	
	25th		Commencement of complete reorganisation and re-equipping of "A" and "D" Companies.	
	26th		Readjustment and partial withdrawal of 174 and 175 Infantry Brigade Frontages - in order to form a stronger defensive flank to the N. along RIVER OISE	
			<u>NEW DISPOSITION</u>	
			"B" Company. 8 Guns with 174 Brigade	
			8 Guns on Canal Defense S.W of BAC D'ARBLINCOURT.	
			Company H.Q. BAC D'ARBLINCOURT.	
			"C" Company. 8 Guns with 175 Brigade.	
			8 Guns on MANICAMP - LE BAC D'ARBLINCOURT defences.	
			Company H.Q. BESME.	
	27th		Battalion H.Q. - A. Company - D Company from BESME to CAMELIN.	
	28th		Battalion H.Q - A. Company - D Company from CAMELIN to BLERANCOURT.	
	29th }		Battalion H.Q BLERANCOURT.	
	30th }		"A" and "D" Companies (re-equipped with Vickers Guns) in training.	[signature]
	31st }			

D. D. & L., London, E.C.
(A8004) Wt. W1771/M2 31 750,000 5/17 Sch. 52 Forms/C2118/14

APPENDIX N° I.

WAR DIARY

or

~~INTELLIGENCE SUMMARY.~~

(Erase heading not required.)

Army Form C. 2118.

Instructions regarding War Diaries and Intelligence Summaries are contained in F. S. Regs., Part II. and the Staff Manual respectively. Title pages will be prepared in manuscript.

Place	Date	Hour	Summary of Events and Information	Remarks and references to Appendices
58TH DIVISIONAL SECTOR. astride RIVER OISE	20th	3.0.pm	Order to "Take Precautionary action"	
	21st		Enemy attacked on a wide front, his left flank resting on the RIVER OISE. This owing to the existing dispositions of the Division the 173rd INFANTRY BRIGADE and A M.G.Coy (with its attached Section from "D" Coy) became heavily engaged – while no attack developed against the two Brigades South of the River, nor was the Centre Brigade able to assist the Northern Brigade in any way – owing to the wide marsh separating the two Sectors.	
		4.45.a.m.	about 4.45.a.m. heavy enemy shelling (including gas shells) commenced on the TERGNIER sector, and	
		9.0.a.m	by 9.a.m. the enemy were reported to be attacking. A dense mist prevented any observation of enemy movements.	
		10.a.m	at about 10.a.m. O.C. "A" Company having received information that the enemy was surrounding ST FIRMIN KEEP, sent 3 Reserve Guns (attached from "D" Coy) under 2nd Lieut O.P. PRATT, to a position E of QUESSY whence fire was brought to bear on an area some 1200x E. of FARGNIERS. with the object of preventing the enemy from advancing on to FARGNIERS (3000 rounds were fired on this task).	
		11.a.m.	at 11.0.a.m. O.C "A" Company received information by runner from one of his forward Sections, that 2nd Lieut T. OWEN – who was with two of the forward guns, had been taken prisoner, the enemy enveloping these two guns in the mist – but that one of the guns had been got away and moved to a position near LA FERME ROUGE – where 2 other guns were in position. This position was then attacked by the enemy – very large numbers advancing astride the LA FÈRE – LIEZ ROAD. Heavy fire was opened which held the enemy off for two hours, inflicting very heavy casualties. These guns were eventually withdrawn to a position just E. of QUESSY – in order to get enfilade fire on the advancing enemy, a Company of 2/4th LONDON REGIMENT was in position at this place.	
		12 noon	By 12 noon two Machine Guns on the CANAL BANK, S.E of FARGNIERS and others E. of FARGNIERS and QUESSY were engaging hostile infantry at Close range.	
		1.p.m.	at 1. pm. a Corporal in charge of one of the foremost guns arrived at "A" Co. H.Q. and reported that his gun had held out until 12.15.p.m. when it was eventually put out of action by hostile M.G. fire. The enemy are stated to have suffered very heavy casualties from this gun, which was eventually almost surrounded.	[signature]

D. D. & L., London, E.C.
(A8004) Wt. W1771/M2031 750,000 5/17 Sch. 52 Forms/C2118/14

Instructions regarding War Diaries and Intelligence Summaries are contained in F. S. Regs., Part II. and the Staff Manual respectively. Title pages will be prepared in manuscript.

WAR DIARY

or

~~INTELLIGENCE SUMMARY.~~

(Erase heading not required.)

Army Form C. 2118.

Place	Date	Hour	Summary of Events and Information	Remarks and references to Appendices
		1.p.m.	Two guns on the Canal Bank S.E. of FARGNIERS under 16040 Sgt. J.W. TANN held out against three big attacks (delivered from the S.E) until 7.p.m. the enemy eventually digging in about 150 yards away in front of the wire.	
		7.30. p.m.	Owing to the penetration of the enemy to the NORTH these guns were withdrawn with the Infantry down the Southern Bank of the Canal, taking up positions in conjunction with the Infantry at the junction of the CROZART and St QUENTIN CANALS.	
			Shortly before dusk O.C. "A" Coy was ordered by G.O.C. 173rd Brigade to withdraw all guns from the Battle Zone and to hold the W. Bank of the CROZART CANAL at all costs throughout the night of 21st/22nd.	
			This was done with 8 Guns, which remained out of the 19 Guns originally under "A" Coy.	
			As regards the other guns of which no detailed information can be given, many reports are given of heavy casualties inflicted by their fire until overwhelmed or destroyed.	
			Situation as regards "B" and "C" M.G. Companies unchanged.	
	Night. 21/22		"A" Coy with 8 guns holding CANAL as above.	
		10.30p.m.	At 10.30.p.m. orders were received by Battalion H.Q from Division for 1 Section "D" Company attached to 174 Brigade and 1 Section "D" Coy attached 175 Brigade to move immediately, and to establish themselves on the GREEN LINE on the front LES QUARTRE CHEMINS (VIRY NOUREUIL ROAD) - BUTTES de VOUEL (VOUEL - ROUEZ Road) both inclusive.	
		5.30. a.m.	One of these Sections took up the positions allotted to them - being in position about 5.30.a.m 22nd. The other Section was not put into position as the dismounted cavalry who were moved up the same night to hold the Green Line had an abundance of M.G's with them. This Section was therefore kept in reserve in VIRY NOUREUIL.	
			A third Section of "D" Company was moved up during the evening of 21st and took up position in some quarries about 1500x due W of QUESSY.	[illegible]

D. D. & L., London, E.C. (A8004) Wt. W1771/M2931 750,000 5/17 Sch. 52 Forms/C2118/14

Instructions regarding War Diaries and Intelligence Summaries are contained in F. S. Regs., Part II. and the Staff Manual respectively. Title pages will be prepared in manuscript.

WAR DIARY
or
~~INTELLIGENCE SUMMARY.~~
(Erase heading not required.)

Army Form C. 2118.

Place	Date	Hour	Summary of Events and Information	Remarks and references to Appendices
	22ND	2.30 p.m	The dispositions remained as above throughout the morning of 22nd inst.	
			About 2.30. p.m the enemy renewed his attack and succeeded in crossing the CROZART CANAL W. of QUESSY. and in advancing N. of TERGNIER. He then extended his crossings over the CANAL to opposite TERGNIER.	
			Here 6 of the 8 Guns of "A" Company holding the CANAL came into action - the teams firing their guns until the ammunition was exhausted or the guns put out of action by the hostile	
		3.30 p.m	shelling. - this about 3.30. p.m (one of these 6 guns was got away after using all its ammunition)	
			The other 2 out of the 8 Guns were the 2 Guns under Sgt TANN which were withdrawn the previous evening and which were in position at the junction of the CROZART and ST QUENTIN CANALS.	
		3.30 to 7.30 p.m.	These 2 Guns again held their position until about 7.30. p.m 22nd, and by enfilading the CROZART CANAL, E of TERGNIER. accounted for a considerable number of the enemy, though the position they actually held was not attacked.	
			After all the guns of "A" Company, except the two above-mentioned, were out of action (3.30 p.m) Major PULLAR with 2ND LIEUT. WALKER and about 30 Machine Gunners held out in TERGNIER preventing the enemy from getting into the Southern part of the town until 7.0 p.m when O.C. "A" Company was ordered to withdraw all remaining guns and men of his Company to the GREEN LINE and finally about 10. p.m to withdraw to OGNES where the M.G. Transport	
		10.0 p.m	of "A" and "D" Companies was, and to reorganise there. Three guns out of the original 19 still remained.	
			During the afternoon and evening of this day (22nd) the enemy penetrated the line N. of TERGNIER to a depth of some 3000 yards and was pressing Southwards.	
			The 4 Guns of "D" Company in position 1500x W of QUESSY were probably overwhelmed late on 22nd inst	C.O. [illegible]

D. D. & L., London, E.C.
(A8004) Wt. W1771/M2131 750,000 5/17 Sch. 52 Forms/C2118/14

Instructions regarding War Diaries and Intelligence Summaries are contained in F. S. Regs., Part II. and the Staff Manual respectively. Title pages will be prepared in manuscript.

WAR DIARY
or
~~INTELLIGENCE SUMMARY.~~
(Erase heading not required.)

Army Form C. 2118.

Place	Date	Hour	Summary of Events and Information	Remarks and references to Appendices
			The 4 Guns of "D" Company just S. of BUTTE de VOUEL however were holding out and engaged many enemy targets including enemy cavalry.	
		9.0 p.m.	At 9.p.m a limber with rations and 20000 rounds S.A.A got through to these 4 guns and they were then all intact but had used almost all their ammunition.	
		8.p.m	At 8.p.m 4 reserve Guns of "D" Company in VIRY NOUREUIL were placed in position. 2 guns on Eastern outskirts of the village and 2 guns on the CANAL about the crossing of the VIRY-CONDREN Road over the Canal.	
		night 22/23rd	Situation unchanged.	
	23rd	7.a.m.	At 7.a.m. 23rd French Troops counter attacked from a line running North from VIRY-NOUREUIL - TERGNIER Road. This counter attack passed over our troops still holding the Green Line and seems to have reached about the line of the VOUEL - CONDREN Road.	
		9.30.a.m	At 9.30.a.m. the 4 Guns just S. of BUTTE de VOUEL were still intact.	
			Following the counter attack by the French the enemy again pushed a strong attack through the N. of TERGNIER penetrating far into the BOIS DE FRIERES and pressed strongly SOUTHWARDS on to the NORTH OF NOUREUIL.	
			The defence of the Green Line and NOUREUIL once more fell upon the remnants of the 173rd Brigade and the dismounted cavalry.	
			The 4 Guns of "D" Company S of BUTTE de VOUEL were probably overwhelmed about midday 23rd.	
			It is certain that these Guns did great execution amongst the Enemy and that Lieut F.H. BAKER and Lieut A.P.S. BORTHWICK, held their position for about 30 hours.	[initials]

D. D. & L., London, E.C.
(A8004) Wt. W1771/M2-31 750,000 5/17 Sch. 52 Forms/C2118/14

Instructions regarding War Diaries and Intelligence Summaries are contained in F. S. Regs., Part II. and the Staff Manual respectively. Title pages will be prepared in manuscript.

WAR DIARY
or
~~INTELLIGENCE SUMMARY.~~
(Erase heading not required.)

Army Form C. 2118.

Place	Date	Hour	Summary of Events and Information	Remarks and references to Appendices
		11.a.m	At 11.a.m the 4 Guns of D Company E. of VIRY NOUREUIL were engaged with targets of enemy Infantry and held their positions until 2 of the Guns (on the Canal Bank) were put out of action by hostile shelling during the afternoon.	
		1.p.m	At 1.p.m 1 Gun of "A" Company under Lieut O.P. PRATT was sent up from OGNES to take up position E. of CHAUNY with the object of holding the enemy in his advance on CHAUNY especially from the N. and N.E.	
			NOUREUIL and VIRY NOUREUIL were still holding out.	
	Night. 23/24		The defence of VIRY and VIRY NOUREUIL ~~was taken~~ over by the French on the evening of 23rd, when the two remaining guns were withdrawn to the CHAUNY defences.	
	24th	11.a.m	The two guns in the CHAUNY Line were put out of action about 11.a.m 24th after having been engaged with hostile Infantry and Cavalry throughout the morning.	
			Lieut O.P. PRATT held his position E. of CHAUNY until the French took over this line, when he withdrew with the remainder of the Infantry, rejoining "A" Company at BESME about 10.a.m 25th.	

SUMMARY OF CASUALTIES 21-24.3.1918.

21.3.1918	2nd Lt. T. Owen. Prisoner of War.	21.3.1918	2. O. Ranks	Killed
"	" A. Deale Wounded.	"	6 "	Wounded
"	" A.P.S. Borthwick, Wounded.	"	26 "	Missing
"	" A.C. Heggs. Wounded (Gas)	22.3.1918	1 "	Killed
"	" T.C. Forman " "	"	2 "	Wounded
"	Capt J.S. Palliser Wounded (Remained at Duty)	"	17 "	Missing
24.3.1918	2nd Lt. F.H. Baker. Missing believed P. of W	24.3.1918	1 "	Wounded
"	" E.P. Martin " "	"	44 "	Missing
"	" J. Robertson. Missing.	"	5 " (attached) "	

[signature]

D. D. & L., London, E.C.
(A8004) Wt. W1771/M2131 750,000 5/17 Sch. 52 Forms/C2118/14

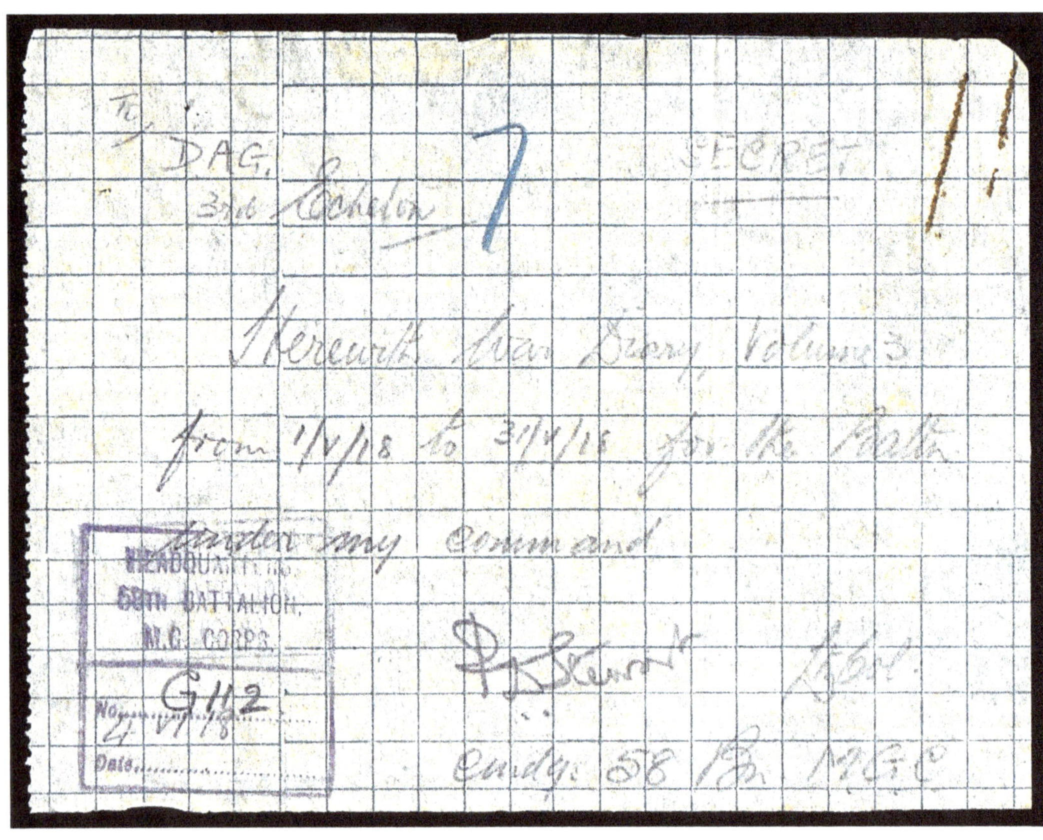

To/ D.A.G.
3rd Echelon

7

SECRET

Herewith War Diary Volume 3
from 1/V/18 to 31/V/18 for the Battn
under my command

HEADQUARTERS
58th BATTALION,
M.G. CORPS.
No. G112
Date 4 VI/18

P. J. Stewart Lt Col
Cmdg. 58 Bn. M.G.C.

7 55 Army Form C. 2118.

WAR DIARY
or
INTELLIGENCE SUMMARY.
(*Erase heading not required.*)

Instructions regarding War Diaries and Intelligence Summaries are contained in F. S. Regs., Part II. and the Staff Manual respectively. Title pages will be prepared in manuscript.

Paget.

58th. Battn. M.G.C.
Volume No. 3.

Vol 3

Place	Date	Hour	Summary of Events and Information	Remarks and references to Appendices
	1918			
YAUCOURT-BUSSES	MAY	1st.	Re-equipment of men & programme of training carried out	
		2nd.	Lt. SMALLWOOD (Signalling Officer) & 80 OR reinforcements arrived from Base.	
			Training of Companies continued	
		3rd.	Training	
		4.	Battalion Route March and inspection of transport	
		5.	Church parades. Battn. Transport moved off by road to BOURDON where they stayed the night. 7 Officers (2/Lts. BROOKS, ASTBURY, GRAYSON, WEST, STEVENS, TOWNSEND, & Lt. BANKS) joined from Base Depot.	Sheet 17 AMIENS.
MIRVAUX		6.	Battalion less D Company, moved by bus to MOLLIENS AU BOIS and marched to MIRVAUX where billets were occupied.	Sheet 62 D; Sheet 57 D
			D Company moved by bus to CONTAY and marched to BAISIEUX.	Sheet 62 D
			Capt. FERRIE, O.C. D Company, reconnoitred line WARLOY - FRANVILLERS (embracing BAISIEUX Defences).	Sheets 57 D and 62 D
			Transport less that of D Company moved from BOURDON to MIRVAUX	
		7.	D Company H.Q. at Chateau BAIZIEUX and company occupied position in BAIZIEUX Defences.	
			Battn. H.Q., A. B. & C. Companies moved from MIRVAUX & billeted at MOLLIENS AU BOIS	Sheet 62 D.
MOLLIENS AU BOIS		8.	A. B. & C. Companies carrying out training programmes.	
			A. & C. Companies affiliated to 173 & 174 Bdes. for counter-attack in the event	

D. D. & L., London, E.C. (A8004) Wt. W1771/M2031 750,000 5/17 Sch. 52 Forms/C2118/14

Army Form C. 2118.

WAR DIARY
or
INTELLIGENCE SUMMARY.
(Erase heading not required.)

Instructions regarding War Diaries and Intelligence Summaries are contained in F. S. Regs., Part II. and the Staff Manual respectively. Title pages will be prepared in manuscript.

Page 2

Place	Date	Hour	Summary of Events and Information	Remarks and references to Appendices
MOLLIENS AU BOIS	1918 MAY		of an enemy attack. B Company reserve.	
		8.	Capt. DREW, C. Company, reconnoitred Left Divl. Sector, BAISIEUX System & valleys in C5 and U29 in conjunction with 174 Bde. Group.	Sheets 62D } — 57D }
			Lt E.J. DOWLEY and 77 O.R. reinforcements from Base.	
		9.	A & C Companies moved to C.20.b.3.6. and C.8.a.6.2 respectively	Sheet 62D See Appendix F.
			D Company relieved & moved back to MOLLIENS AU BOIS & affiliated to 173 Bde.	
			34 M.G. Battn. took over BAISIEUX Defence Line.	
		10.	Programme of training carried out by B & D Companies. A & C Companies in Bivouacs	
			Major D. RALSTON joined as Second in Command of Battn.	
			Percentage of B & D Companies & H.Q. inoculated.	
		11	Training	
		12	Lt J.H. CAESAR, 2/Lt C.P.L. WATTS, Lt C.M. COATES & 2/Lt C. RICHARDSON transferred from 18 Battn. M.G.C. & posted to A. B & D Companies.	
			Lt E.J. DOWLEY transferred from D to C Company.	
			Imprest a/c M.G.C. 526 opened for Battn. H.Q.	
			Church parades for B & D Companies.	
		13.	2/Lt G.S. TOWNSEND rejoined from Course. 1 C.Q.M.S. joined from Base.	
			Training	
		14.	Tactical Scheme carried out by B. Company.	

R. Stewart Lt Col

D. D. & L., London, E.C. (A8004) Wt. W1771/M2031 750,000 5/17 Sch. 52 Forms/C2118/14

Army Form C. 2118.

WAR DIARY
or
INTELLIGENCE SUMMARY.
(Erase heading not required.)

Instructions regarding War Diaries and Intelligence Summaries are contained in F. S. Regs., Part II. and the Staff Manual respectively. Title pages will be prepared in manuscript.

Place	Date 1918	Hour	Summary of Events and Information	Remarks and references to Appendices
MOLLIENS AU BOIS	MAY	14.	Gas appliances inspection by D.G.O. for D & C. Companies & H.Q. A Coy. training	
		15.	B. Company marched to WARLOY.	Sheet 57 D.
			O.s.C. A.B. & C. Companies reconnoitred line to be relieved from 47th Bn. M.G.C.	Appendix B
		16.	58 Division relieved 47 Division in left Divisional Sector on III Corps front, holding the line from W21a to E2a inclusive.	Sheets 57 D & 62 D
			B Company moved from WARLOY into line relieved A Company 47 Bn. M.G.C in Right Sub-sector with 16 Guns.	
			C Company moved from C.8.a.6.2 into line relieved D Company 47 Bn. M.G.C	Sheet 62 D
			Rear H.Q. & Transport of B Coy. remained at WARLOY. C. Coy. transport at C.8.a.	
			Relief complete without casualties reported by 6.30 am 17th. inst.	Appendix C
			D Company moved to WARLOY & took over billets vacated by B Company. Transport lines at WARLOY. Two sections of D Company relieved 2 Sections of C. Company 47 Bn. M.G.C. in HAM Redoubt (V.23.a & b).	Sheet 57 D
			Bn. T.O. arranged to take over Tpt lines of 47 Bn. at CONTAY	— " —
		17.	Battn. H.Q. closed at MOLLIENS & opened at CONTAY, 10.30 am.	— " —
CONTAY			A Company relieved B Company of 47 Bn. M.G.C. in left sub. sector. No casualties.	
			All Company Transport (less D) moved to CONTAY to lines vacated by 47 Bn. M.G.C	R. Stannard[?] Lt. Col.

D. D. & L., London, E.C. (A8004) Wt. W1771/M2031 750,000 5/17 Sch. 52 Forms/C2118/14

Army Form C. 2118.

Instructions regarding War Diaries and Intelligence Summaries are contained in F. S. Regs., Part II. and the Staff Manual respectively. Title pages will be prepared in manuscript.

Page 4.

WAR DIARY
or
INTELLIGENCE SUMMARY.
(Erase heading not required.)

Place	Date	Hour	Summary of Events and Information	Remarks and references to Appendices
	1918.			
CONTAY	May	18	Situation normal. Companies disposed as follows:-	
			A. 16 guns in forward area	Sheets 57D
			B. 16 guns in right reserve	& 62D.
			C. 16 guns in reserve line	
			D. 8 guns in HAM Redoubt. 8 guns in Div. reserve at WARLOY.	
			A Company had a gun damaged by shell fire & 2 O.R. wounded	
			Forward areas intermittently shelled during the day & back areas bombed at night.	
			Lt. G.L. ROWE, 2/Lt I.E. PEART, 2/Lt F.W. STEADMAN, 2/Lt R. HENDERSON & 30 O.R. joined ~~from~~	Appendix D
		19.	Regrouping of guns took place as follows:-	Sheet 57D
			A Coy. 10 guns in position. 6 guns withdrawn in Reserve at HENENCOURT WOOD	
			B – . 16 guns in line	
			C – . 10 guns in position. 6 guns withdrawn in Reserve at HENENCOURT WOOD	– " –
			D . 4 guns in position. 4 guns in Mobile Reserve at HAM Redoubt	
			8 guns at WARLOY.	
			In the case of attack:-	
			(1) One Section of D Company at disposal of B.G.C. 173 Bde	
			(2) — " — C — " — 174 Bde	
			(3) — " — A — " — 175 Bde	

D. D. & L., London, E.C. (A8001) Wt. W1771/M2031 750,000 5/17 Sch. 52 Forms/C2118/14

Army Form C. 2118.

WAR DIARY
or
INTELLIGENCE SUMMARY.
(*Erase heading not required.*)

Instructions regarding War Diaries and Intelligence Summaries are contained in F. S. Regs., Part II. and the Staff Manual respectively. Title pages will be prepared in manuscript.

Page 5.

Place	Date 1918	Hour	Summary of Events and Information	Remarks and references to Appendices
CONTAY	May	19	Some gas shelling reported & A. Coy had 2 OR wounded.	
			2 OR strength increase – rejoined from Hospital.	
		20.	Further regrouping of Guns:–	
			A. 12 guns in position. 4 guns in Reserve HENENCOURT WOOD	
			B ——— " ——— ——— " ———	
			C ——— " ——— ——— " ———	
			D 8 guns in HAM Redoubt (4 in position + 4 Mobile Reserve) + 8 guns at WARLOY	
			Situation normal	
		21.	Situation quiet but air observers report signs of impending attack	
			52 OR. reinforcements from Base	
		22.	173 Inf. Bde relieved 175 Inf. Bde. Guns reallotted as follows	Appendix E
			A Coy with 173 Bde. Reserve section at disposal of B.G.C.	
			B – – 174 – ——— " ———	
			C – – 174 –	
			D Coy. 8 guns in HAM Redoubt. 8 guns at WARLOY. One section of which at disposal of B.G.C 175 Bde	
			Casualties – 1 OR Gassed	[illegible signature]

D. D. & L., London, E.C.
(A8004) Wt. W1771/M2031 750,000 5/17 Sch. 52 Forms/C2118/14

Instructions regarding War Diaries and Intelligence Summaries are contained in F. S. Regs., Part II. and the Staff Manual respectively. Title pages will be prepared in manuscript.

Army Form C. 2118.

WAR DIARY
or
INTELLIGENCE SUMMARY.
(Erase heading not required.)

Page 6

Place	Date 1918.	Hour	Summary of Events and Information	Remarks and references to Appendices
CONTAY.	May	23	Situation normal. 1 OR Killed. SI., 1 OR wounded	
		24	D Coy. relieved B Coy. in line – 12 Guns in position 4 in reserve at HENENCOURT WOOD. B Company took over billets vacated by D Coy. at WARLOY	Appendix F
			Capt EMSLIE joined with 21 O.R. from Base	
		25	8 Guns of B Coy relieved 8 Guns of D Coy in HAM Redoubt	Sh 62D
			B Coy's transport moved to WARLOY & D Coy Tpt. with A.T.C. at C.16.c.6.5. Allotment of reserve sections as follows:–	
			Reserve Section of D Coy. to 174 Bde	
			B Coy. – 175 Bde	
			Capt. EMSLIE appointed O.C. D Company	
			Casualties 1 O.R. Killed. Situation normal	
		26	Situation normal	
			A/Capt. W.S FERRIE relinquished acting rank on ceasing to command D. Coy.	
		27.	175 Bde. relieved 174 Bde. & Gun sections reallotted accordingly	[illegible] Lt Col?
			1 Gun of B Company took up position in front line trench about W.21.b.3.3 & successfully carried out harassing fire on railway	Sh 57D

D. D. & L., London, E.C.
(A7001) Wt. W1771/M2031 750,000 5/17 Sch. 52 Forms/C2118/14

Army Form C. 2118.

WAR DIARY
or
INTELLIGENCE SUMMARY.
(Erase heading not required.)

Instructions regarding War Diaries and Intelligence Summaries are contained in F. S. Regs., Part II. and the Staff Manual respectively. Title pages will be prepared in manuscript.

Page 7

Place	Date 1918	Hour	Summary of Events and Information	Remarks and references to Appendices
CONTAY	May	27	embankment S.W. of ALBERT E.3.b. to E.9.d. Vicinity of Battn H.Q. shelled with about 30 H.V. (5.9) no casualties but some damage done to village. 1 OR joined from Base	Sheet 62 D
		28	Considerable hostile aircraft & artillery activity, otherwise situation normal	
		29	Situation unchanged	
		30	Nothing special to report. Usual artillery activity & bombing of back areas at night. 2 OR wounded 2 OR killed in action	
		31	Harassing fire carried out. A.C.&D. Companies fired on SOS lines. 1 Gun B Company fired six belts from W.21.c on Railway embankment E.3.b. to E.9.b. Increase in gas shelling. Bombing in back areas	Sheet 57 D Sheet 62 D
		31.V.18		

R.D. Stewart Lieut Col.
Cmdg. 58 Bn. MGC.

(Appendices attached to original copy only)

D. D. & L., London, E.C. (A6031) Wt. W1771/M2031 750,000 5/17 Sch. 52 Forms/C2118/14

War Diary

APPENDIX - A.

MOVE ORDERS.

BY LIEUT COL. P.D.STEWART., D.S.O.

COMMANDING 58th BATTALION MACHINE GUN CORPS.

Map Ref. SHEET 62 D.

1. A and C Companies will move to areas in Valley EAST of BAVILLINCOURT and MONTIGNY C 8 a. and c., C 14 a. and c. today the 9th inst.

   D Company will move from BAIZIEUX to MOLLIENS AU BOIS.

   Exact location to be notified later to all concerned.

2. C Company will be clear of MOLLIENS AU BOIS by 2.p.m.

   A Company will be clear by 2.15.p.m.

   D Company will occupy billets at MOLLIENS AU BOIS vacated by A and C Companies.

3. ROUTE.

   C Company BEAUCOURT - BAVILLINCOURT.

   A Company BEAUCOURT - BEHENCOURT.

4. A detachment of Signallers will report to A and C Companies and are responsible for establishing communication by line to 175 Brigade at BAZIEUX.

5. Companies will be in communication to Battalion H.Q. and their respective Brigades via 175 Brigade and 58th Division.

6. Tentage in possession at present will be taken by A and C Companies to their new location.

   D Company will bring their own tentage to MOLLIENS AU BOIS.

7. S.A.A.

   40000 rounds S.A.A. is dumped at C 11 a. 8. 4.

War Diary appendix B.

SECRET. **OPERATION ORDERS NO. 7.** Copy No. 12

BY LIEUT COL. F.D. STEWART, D.S.O.

COMMANDING 58th BATTALION MACHINE GUN CORPS.

Map Ref. Sheet 57 D. S.W. and S.E. 1.20000
" 62 D. N.W. and N.E. 1.20000

May 14th 1918.

1. The 58th DIVISION will relieve the 47th DIVISION on the nights 15/16th and 16/17th inst and be disposed as follows:-
   Right Sub-Sector 174th Infantry Brigade.
   Left Sub-Sector 175th Infantry Brigade.
   Divisional Reserve. 173rd Infantry Brigade.

2. 3 Companies of this Battalion will relieve and be disposed as under:-
   B Coy. will relieve A Co. 47th Bn with 16 guns on night 16/17th.
   C.Coy will relieve D Co. 47th Bn with 16 guns on night 16/17th.
   A Coy. will relieve B Co. 47th Bn with 16 guns on night 17/18th.
   D Coy will move to C 8 a. to bivouac camp at present occupied by C Coy on morning of 16th.

3. Officers Commanding Companies will make the usual arrangements for relief with their opposite numbers.

4. The following stores will be taken over from 47th Battalion at gun positions:-
   12 belt boxes, filled belts, per gun.
   S.A.A. not less than 10 boxes per gun.
   T. Base platforms.
   Battery Charts and Fire Orders.
   Petrol tins with water, 2 per gun.
   Camouflage at present over gun emplacements.

5. Company Commanders will arrange to hand over to 47th Battalion Companies at WARLOY.
   12 belt boxes filled belts per gun.
   2 petrol tins per gun.

   and take up sufficient filled belts and boxes to make a total of 20 per gun at each gun position; also further petrol tins as required.

6. Guides will meet B and C Companies at 9 p.m. on night 16/17th at V 27 d. 3.8. (Junction of WARLOY - HENENCOURT and BAIZIEUX - HENENCOURT ROADS).

   O.C. A. Company will make his own arrangements for guides on night 17/18th.

7. Company Commanders will arrange for their Section Officers to reconnoitre their areas and O.C. "C" Company will meet O.C. "D" Company, 47th Battalion between 9 and 10 a.m. on morning of 16th inst at the latter Company's H.Q. at HENENCOURT V 27 b. 5.5. approx.

   O.C. "A" Company will get in touch with O.C. "B" Company 47th Battalion Company H.Q. W 10 d. 8. 2. for the same purpose.

8. B Company will be billeted in WARLOY on night 15/16th. A and C Companies will move direct from their present camps.

9. Transport will be under Company arrangements in localities W of WARLOY

10. O.C.Signals will arrange with his opposite number to take over the present systems of communication and exchange the material taken over.

11. Company Commanders will see that their Section Officers each have a 1/20000 map of their areas and notify their requirements by 12 noon 15th inst.

12. Reliefs will be reported to Battalion H.Q. (locality to be notified later) by Code Word <u>BEER.</u>

T.WATKINS. 2nd Lt. and Adjt.

Copy No. 1. 58th DIV.G
2. 58th DIV Q.
3. 173.INF.BDE.
4. 174. INF BDE.
5. 175 INF BDE.
6. O.C.58th Bn.M.G.C.
6a. 47th DIV.
6b. 47th Bn. M.G.C.
7. O.C. "A" Co.
8. O.C."B" Co.
9. O.C."C" Co.
10. O.C."D" Co.
11. O.C.58th Bn.M.G.C.Signals.
12. War Diary.
13. File.

SECRET. War Diary OPERATION ORDER No.8. Copy No 16.

BY LIEUT COL. P.D.STEWART., D.S.O.

COMMANDING 58th BATTALION MACHINE GUN CORPS. Appendix C.

Map Ref. SHEETS.

57 D. S.W. & S.E. 1:20000. 15th May 1918.

62 D. N.W. & N.E. 1.20000.

1. "D" Company will move to WARLOY tomorrow the 16th inst and take over Billets vacated by "B" Company - not to arrive in WARLOY before 6.30. Company cooker to go on in advance and have tea ready on arrival.

2. O.C. "D" Company will detail two complete Sections to take over gun positions on night 16/17th from 47th Bn M.G.C. and make all necessary arrangements for the relief with his opposite number "C" These guns will be located in V 23 b, and must be specially warned about keeping the position quiet by day.

3. The Transport Officer will arrange to take over the Transport Lines at CONTAY with any tents, shelters, etc vacated by the 47th Bn, and if suitable all the Company transport will be located there with exception of D Company, which will be at WARLOY.

4. The Q.M. will arrange for the taking over of all Battalion and Co Q.M. Store Billets vacated by the 47th Bn at CONTAY, and Company Q.M. Stores will be at this place, with the exception of D Company, which will be at WARLOY.

T.WATKINS 2nd Lt and Adjt.

War Diary Copy.

War Diary. Appendix D

SECRET.

OPERATION ORDER No.9.
BY LIEUT COL.P.D.STEWART.D.S.O.
COMMANDING 58th BATTALION MACHINE GUN CORPS.

Map Ref. SHEET 57.D. S.E 1:20000. May 18th 1918.

1. The following gun positions will be abandoned tonight:-

   No 12 Battery. C. Company guns.
   No 13 Battery C Company Guns.

   O.C. "C" Company will arrange to take over from "A" Company, the gun positions at No 18 Battery, thus releasing one Section from each Company.

2. O.C. "C" Company will place two guns of No 17 Battery in position in THE MAZE selecting the most suitable sites; the remaining two guns of No 17 occupying the best sites in Nos 12 and 17 Battery positions.

3. O.C. "D" Company will withdraw one Section, which will be maintained as mobile Battery in HAN REDOUBT but not in position. The remaining Section will have two guns in each of the positions at present occupied, one pair to fire in a Northerly direction the other pair in an Easterly direction.

   The relieved Sections of A, B and C will be located in vicinity of HENENCOURT WOOD.

4. The relieved sections of A, B and C Companies will bring away with them all stores at gun positions, and as much S.A.A. as possible, handing over what they are unable to carry out to one of their other batteries, to be removed later.

Copy No 1 to 58.DIV. G.
2. 173. INF.BDE.
3. 174 INF. BDE.
4. 175 INF. BDE.
5. A.Co.
6. B.Co.
7. C.Co.
8. D Co.
9. O.C.58 Bn.M.G.C.
10. War Diary.
11. File.

T.WATKINS 2nd Lt & Adjt.

War Diary

SECRET. **AMENDMENT TO OPERATION ORDER No.9.** Copy No. 10
BY LIEUT.COL F.R.STEWART., D.S.O.
COMMANDING 58th BATTALION MACHINE GUN CORPS.

Map Ref: SHEET 57 D. S.E. 1:20000 19th May 1918.

1. In para 3, sub para 2 delete "B" and read as follows:-

Relieved Sections of A and C will be located in vicinity of HENENCOURT WOOD.

2. In para 4 delete "B" and read

A and C Companies will bring away etc.

Copy No 1. 58 DIV G.
2. 173 INF BDE.
3. 174 INF BDE.
4. 175 INF BDE.
5. A Co.
6. B Co.
7. C. Co.
8. D.Co.
9. O.C.58 Bn M.G.C.
10. War Diary.
11. File.

T.WATKINS 2nd Lt & Adjt.

War Diary Appendix E

Copy No. 10

ORDER No 10.
BY LIEUT COL. T.D.STEWART., D.S.O.
COMMANDING 58th BATTALION MACHINE GUN CORPS.

Map Ref. 57 D and 62 D. 1:20000.

On relief of 175 Infantry Brigade, Reserve Sections of this Battalion will be as under:-

Reserve Section of "A" Company will be at disposal of G.O.C. 173rd INFANTRY BRIGADE; Reserve Section of "B" Company at disposal of 174th INFANTRY BRIGADE; One Section of "D" Company, WARLOY, at disposal of 175th INFANTRY BRIGADE.

In the event of attack or counter-attack, Officers Commanding Companies will report as above to their respective Brigades giving the name of Section Officer, and ascertaining the probable intentions of Brigadier Generals as to their employment.

Copy No. 1. 58 DIV G.
2. O.C.58 Bn.
3. 173 Bde.
4. 174 Bde.
5. 175 Bde.
6. O.C.A.Co.
7. O.C. B Co.
8. O.C.C.Co.
9. O.C.D.Co.
10. War Diary. ✓
11. File.

T.WATKINS 2nd Lieut & Adjt

SECRET. ORDER NO 11. COPY NO. 10

Appendix F.

BY LIEUT COL. F. D. STEWART., [illegible]

COMMANDING 58th BATTALION MACHINE GUN CORPS.

Map Ref. SHEET 57 D. 1.20000. 24th [illegible] 1918.

1. D Company will relieve B Company in the Right Sub-Sector (174th Infantry Brigade) on night 25/26th inst.

2. Details for the relief will be arranged between Company Commanders concerned.

3. On relief D Company's Transport will move to [illegible] in [illegible] 10 c.3.5. (where A and C Company's Transport are)

4. B Company's Transport will take over D Company's lines at [illegible]LOY.

4. For the reserve section of D Company at [illegible] pack mules will be kept and NOT limbers.

6. On relief complete, Company Commanders will notify their respective Brigades giving name of Section Officer of Reserve Section

8. Relief complete will be wired to this Office by Code Word VICTORIA.

7. ACKNOWLEDGE.

(Distribution over) T. [illegible] 2nd Lt and Adjt.

Copy No 1. 58 DIV G.

2. 173 Bde.

3 174 Bde.

4 175 Bde.

5 O.C. 58 Bn M.G.C.

6. A. Co.
7. B. Co.

8. C. Co.

9. D. Co.

10. War Diary.

11. File.

SECRET.
D.A.G. 3rd Echelon. 4

Herewith original War Diary, Volume4, of the Battalion under my command, for the month of June 1918.

R D Stewart Lieut Col.

1.7.18 cmdg 58 Battalion M.G.C.

58

Instructions regarding War Diaries and Intelligence Summaries are contained in F. S. Regs., Part II. and the Staff Manual respectively. Title pages will be prepared in manuscript.

WAR DIARY

~~or~~

~~INTELLIGENCE SUMMARY.~~

(Erase heading not required.)

58th Battalion Machine Gun Corps

June 1st - 30th

Volume 4

Army Form C. 2118.

Vol 4

Place	Date	Hour	Summary of Events and Information	Remarks and references to Appendices
CONTAY	1st		B, C & D Coys relieved by B, D & C Coys respectively of 18th Batt MGC	Appendix A
			B Coy moved to C 20d 99.	Sheet 62D
			C " " MIRVAUX	Sheet 57D
			D " " C 8a.	Sheet 62D
			35th Div on the left carried out minor operation on AVELUY WOOD capturing 77 Prisoners and 6 Machine Guns	
			LIEUT W. S. FERRIE transferred to 51st Batt M.G.C.	
			Reinforcements 7 OR arrived from Base	
MIRVAUX	2nd		BHQ relieved by BHQ 18th Batt MGC	
		12 noon	BHQ closed at CONTAY opened at MIRVAUX	Sheet 57D
			Reinforcements 1 OR arrived from Base	
	3rd		The 58th Div being in CORPS RESERVE the Batt is to be ready to Counter attack in the event of the enemy breaking through. In case of the Batt being ordered to counter attack:-	
			2 secs of D Coy will be attached to 173 Inf Brigade.	
			2 " " D " " " " 175 " "	
			2 " " B " " " " 174 " "	
			The remaining guns will be in Div reserve.	
			A Coy will operate in left Brigade Sector	
			C " " " Right " "	
			B - (less 2 secs) in Mobile Reserve	
			3 OR Evacuated	
	4th		Training carried out	
			1 OR Evacuated.	

D. D. & L., London, E.C. (A8001) Wt. W1771/M2031 750,000 5/17 Sch. 52 Forms/C2118/14

* Instructions regarding War Diaries and Intelligence Summaries are contained in F. S. Regs., Part II. and the Staff Manual respectively. Title pages will be prepared in manuscript.

WAR DIARY

~~or~~

~~INTELLIGENCE SUMMARY.~~

(Erase heading not required.)

58th Battalion Machine Gun Corps. June 1st - 30th

Army Form C. 2118.

Place	Date	Hour	Summary of Events and Information	Remarks and references to Appendices
MIRVAUX	5th		B + D Coys moved to MIRVAUX. 1 OR Evacuated. Training carried out by A + C Coys	Sheet 57 D.
	6th		Training carried out.	
		3pm	Demonstration of new Anti-aircraft Pivot mounting to 3rd Corps Commander.	
			58th Division now under command of 22nd Corps in GHQ reserve. Reinforcements 3 OR from Base	
	7th		Training carried out.	
	8th		Training carried out Reinforcements 57 OR from Base	
			Capt L.I.L. PULLAR struck off strength.	
	9th		Training Carried out. Inspection of Battalion by Corps Commander. 1 OR reported from Base 1 OR Evacuated.	
	10th		The Battn moved to new area. Transport moved by road. The Coys embussing with the Brigades to which they were affiliated and took over billets	
			BHQ opened at FOURDRINOY	AMIENS 17 1/100.000.
			A Coy at FERRIERES	
			B " " FOURDRINOY	
			C " " SEUX	
			D " " SAVEUSE.	
FOURDRINOY	11th		TRAINING carried out	
			No 2 & 4 Secs of C Coy and 16 Lewis Guns from 175 Inf Brigade formed a mobile detachment under Capt W.R. HOLLAND located at PISSY and under direct orders of 175 Inf Brigade	

A7092 Wt. W1289/M1293. 750,000. 1/17. D. D & L., Ltd. Forms/C2118/14.

Instructions regarding War Diaries and Intelligence Summaries are contained in F. S. Regs., Par. II. and the Staff Manual respectively. Title pages will be prepared in manuscript.

WAR DIARY
~~INTELLIGENCE~~ SUMMARY.
(*Erase heading not required.*)

58th Battalion Machine Gun Corps June 1st - 30th

Army Form C. 2118.

Place	Date	Hour	Summary of Events and Information	Remarks and references to Appendices
FOUDRINOY	12th		Training Carried out. The mobile detachment of C Coy rejoined the unit	AMIENS 17 1/100,000
	13th		Training Carried out 2nd Lt WELLS evacuated.	
	14th		Training Carried out 1 OR Evacuated	
	15th		Training Carried out 3 OR Evacuated	
			2Lts 7A SCOTT, CE SEARLE, FG HARVEY R THOMAS, HT SWAN joined from Base	
	16th		A + D Coys marched to FOUDRINOY and were billeted for the night	
			Transport of A + D Coys moved by road to new area	
	17th		Batt HQ closed at FOUDRINOY opened in wood SE of MOLLIENS aux BOIS	
			A Coy embussed to new area taking over billets at EBARTS FARM from 47th Batt MGC	57 D.
		130pm	B Coy embussed to new area quartered in tents in wood SE of MOLLIENS aux BOIS	
			B Coy transport moved by road to new area	Appendix B
			D Coy embussed to BAIZIEUX No 1 2 3 4 sections moved to position in Support Line	
			relieving D Coy of 47th Batt MGC	
MOLLIENS aux BOIS. WOOD	18th		C Coy (less transport) embussed to new area taking over the tents of B Coy in wood SE	
			MOLLIENS aux BOIS. Transport proceeded by road	
			A Coy relieved C Coy 47th Batt MGC in left sub sector	

A6945 Wt. W11422/M1160 350,000 12/16 D. D. & L. Forms/C./2118/14.

Instructions regarding War Diaries and Intelligence Summaries are contained in F. S. Regs., Part II. and the Staff Manual respectively. Title pages will be prepared in manuscript.

WAR DIARY

~~INTELLIGENCE SUMMARY.~~

(*Erase heading not required.*)

58th Battalion
Machine Gun Corps
June 1st - 30th

Army Form C. 2118.

Place	Date	Hour	Summary of Events and Information	Remarks and references to Appendices
MOLLIENS aux BOIS	18th	7pm	B Coy moved in to EBARTS FARM taking over billets vacated by A Coy	57 D.
			D Coy into Support line	
EBARTS FARM.	19th	6pm	BHQ closed at MOLLIENS aux BOIS WOOD and opened at EBARTS FARM	57 D C.i.c.
			A Coy in line	
		7pm	B Coy took over support line from D Coy	
			C Coy moves to vicinity of EBARTS FARM In reserve	B 6 central
			D Coy relieved A Coy 47th Batt. MGC in Right Sub sector	
	20th		ABD Coys in line. C Coy carried out training	
			A.B. Coys rear HQ in BEAUCOURT. D Coy at BAIZIEUX. 2 OR wounded	
	21st		A.B.D Coys in line C Coy carried out training	
			LIEUT ROWE wounded & evacuated 8 OR evacuated 1 OR rejoined from Hospital	
			D Coy rear HQ moved to BEAUCOURT	
	22nd		ABD Coys in line C Coy carried out training 1 OR wounded.	
	23rd		ABD Coys in line C Coy carried out training 1 OR rejoined from hospital	
	24th		ABD Coys in line C Coy carried out training Capt R.W. KEMP wounded remained at duty	
			Rear Four guns were withdrawn from line of ABD Coys to vicinity of Coy HQ for reserve	
			1 sect of each of A & D Coys held in MOBILE RESERVE at the disposal of their respective Brigade.	

A6945 Wt. W11422/M1160 35,000 12/16 D. D. & L. Forms/C./2118/14.

Instructions regarding War Diaries and Intelligence Summaries are contained in F. S. Regs., Par. II. and the Staff Manual respectively. Title pages will be prepared in manuscript.

WAR DIARY
or
~~INTELLIGENCE SUMMARY.~~
(*Erase heading not required.*)

58th Battn Machine Gun Corps Army Form C. 2118.

June 1st – 30th

Place	Date	Hour	Summary of Events and Information	Remarks and references to Appendices
EBARTS FARM	25th		A B. D Coys in line	57 C N.W.
			C Coy in Reserve carried out training.	
	26th		ABD Coys in line. C Coy in Reserve carried out training	
			B Coy headquarters moved to BOIS ROBERT with 1 section and came under the orders of the 174 Inf Brigade as a mobile section.	
			All remaining guns of AB, D Coys were grouped under two Group Commanders in Left sector and Right sector Group commanders there being 18 guns in each sector and a mobile section at each Inf Brigade HQ.	
	27th		C Coy relieved A Coy in the left sector.	Appendix C.
			A Coy moved to EBARTS FARM in Divisional Reserve. 2nd Lt Trent evacuated sick	
	28th		B C D Coys in line. A Coy in reserve carried out training.	
			5 OR evacuated. 2 OR rejoined from hospital.	
	29th		B C D Coys in line. A Coy in reserve carried out training.	Considerable [illegible] on the night of the [illegible] in the vicinity of EBARTS FARM. 1 [illegible] fell 30 yds from HQ orderly Room + [illegible] pieces penetrating the shelters.
			1 Armourer Sgt joined from Base. 1 OR rejoined from hospital	
	30th		B C D Coys in line. A Coy carried out training	
			Successful minor operation carried out in conjunction with Corps on our left	

A6945 Wt. W11422/M1160 350,000 12/16 D. D. & L. Forms/C./2118/14.

P. D. Stewart Lieut Col
Comdg 58 Battalion M.G.C.

SECRET. **58th BATTALION MACHINE GUN CORPS.** Copy No 13.

Appendix A.

ORDER NO 12.

Ref. Map
Special Sheet SENLIS, 1/20,000. 31st May 1918.

1. 58th Battalion M.G.C. will be relievedcby 18th Battalion M, G, C. on the nights 1/2nd 2/3rd June.

2. Relief will take place in accordance with attached table. Guides and other details will be arranged between Company Commanders concerned.

3. The following stores will be handed over at Gun Positions, receipts being obtained:-
   - 12 Belt boxes (A.P. ammunition inclusive)
   - "T" Bases,
   - Camouflage,
   - S.O.S. Gun Charts,
   - Range Cards,
   - Bombs.

   A seperate certificate in duplicate will be rendered for the following stores handed over:-
   - S.A.A. at Gun Positions,
   - S.A.A. at Company Headquarters,
   - One day's Reserve Rations,
   - Three days Reserve supply of water.

4. Details for work in progress, all defence instructions, special orders and maps will be handed over to the relieving Companies.

5. Working parties will continue up to the last hour prior to the relief when relieving Company will provide numbers of men required. Instructions re working parties must be carefully handed over.

6. Relief complete will be wired to this office, Code Word "BRISTOL".

7. O.C. Signals will arrange with his opposite number to hand over the present systems of communication and effect the necessary exchange.

8. Battalion Headquarters will close at CONTAY 12 noon on the 2nd of June, and re-open at MIRVAUX at same time.

9. O's C Companies will warn all ranks that all deficiencies caused through neglect and lack of discipline will be paid for by individuals. Arrangemets will be made to draw from relieving units a corresponding number of belt boxes and petrol tins to that handed over at gun positions.

10. Companies will march independently to their new area. O.C "B" Company should arrange to take over any tents, shelters etc., vacated by the 18th Bn Company bivouacked at C 20.b. and move them to C 8.a.

11. ACKNOWLEDGE.

T.WATKINS, 2/nd Lt
& Adjt.,
for Lieut Col Commanding 58th Bn M.G.Corps.

DISTRIBUTION,

Copy No			
1.	58th Div "G"	8.	"B" Co. 58th M.G.Bn.
2.	173rd Inf Bde.	9.	"C" Co do
3rd	174th Inf Bde.	10.	"D" Co do
4.	175th Inf Bde.	11.	O.C.Signals, do
5.	O.C.18th M.G.Bn.	12.	Transport Officer 58th M.G.Bn.
6.	O.C.58th M.G.Bn.	13.	War Diary.
7.	"A" Co do	14.	File.

Relief Table overleaf

RELIEF TABLE.

For 58th BATTALION MACHINE GUN CORPS, ORDER No. 12.

Date.	Unit.	Relieved by.	Destination after relief.	Remarks.
1/2 June.	B Coy.	B Coy. 18th Bn.	C 8.a.	Will bivouac in C 8.a. Arrangements as per para 10 (2) [W typed over]
1/2 June	C Coy.	D Coy. 18th Bn.	MIRVAUX.	Advance Party to report to 2nd Lieut BLOMFIELD at 2 p.m. To-morrow near Town Major's Office MIRVAUX.
1/2 June.	D Coy.	C Coy. 18th Bn.	C 8.a.	Arrangements re Tentage will be notified later.
2/3 June.	A Coy.	A Coy. 18th Bn.	MIRVAUX.	Advance Party to report to Battalion H.Q at MIRVAUX at 2.30 p.m. 2nd June.

Appendix B.

SECRET. 58th BATTALION MACHINE GUN CORPS Copy No. 13

ORDER No 13.

Ref. Sheet. SENLIS 1:20000. June 16th 1918.

1. 58 Bn.M.G.C. will relieve 47 Bn.M.G.C. as follows:-
 a. One Company in Reserve Line. } 17th /// 18th
 b. One Company in Reserve at EBARTS FARM) June.
 c. One Company in Left Sub Sector. 18th /// 19th June.
 d. One Company in Right Sub Sector. 19/20th June.

2. Moves to the new area will be made in accordance with 58 Division Administrative Instructions attached and also Instructions issued by respective Brigade Groups.

3. Reliefs will be carried out as under:-

17/18th June. A Company 58 Bn. will relieve B.Co. 47 Bn at EBARTS FARM, taking over their Billets and Lines

D.Company 58 Bn. will relieve D.Company 47 Bn. in Reserve Line (Company H.Q. D 5 c.30.25.)

O's C. Companies will make necessary arrangements regarding relief.

18/19th June. B Company. 58 Bn. will relieve A.Company 58 Bn. at EBARTS FARM, but will not take over Billets. A.Company 58 Bn. will relieve C Company 47 Bn. in Left Sub Sector.

O's.C. Companies will make necessary arrangements re guides, handing over etc.

19/20th June. C Company 58 Bn. will relieve B Company 58 Bn. at EBARTS FARM taking over Billets previously occupied by A.Company 58 Bn.
D.Company 58 Bn. will relieve D Company 58 Bn. in Reserve Line.

D.Company 58 Bn. will relieve A Company 47 Bn. in the Right Sub Sector.

O's C. Companies will make all arrangements re guides, handing over etc.

4. In taking over occupied positions each Company will take in gun, tripod, and 8 belt boxes, spare parts etc, and will take over from 47 Bn:-

 1. All belt boxes, less 8 being taken in.
 2. S.A.A.
 3. Armour piercing and Tracer Ammunition.
 4. Camouflage.
 5. Instructions, range cards, maps, S.O.S. Lines, work done, etc.
 6. Reserve Rations. Numbers of each ration of sugar, tea, biscuits, preserved meat, must be carefully checked. Receipts for this item will be forwarded separately.

All receipts to be forwarded to this Office morning after each relief.

5. On Forward Guns one N.C.O. and 4 men only will man each gun. On Support Guns one N.C.O. and 3 men.
Battle Surplus of 25 men will be accommodated at each Co.H.Q. Remainder of Battle Surplus will remain provisionally at each Rear Co.H.Q.

6. Reconnaissances of guns in ~~Right~~ Left and ~~Left~~ Right Sub Sectors will be carried out by A and D Company Officers on mornings of

~~xxxxxxxxxxxxxxx~~

18th and 19th respectively.

O.C. A Company 58 Bn. will get into touch with O.C. C. Company 47 Bn. at approx. D 3 d. 3.2. (18th inst)

O.C.D.Company 58 Bn will get into touch with O.C. D.Company 47 Bn. at approx. D 21 b. 3.1. (19th inst)

7. Relief complete will be reported by wire to 47 Bn.H.Q. in every case by Code Word "NEW YORK"

8. On completion of Relief A, B, C and D Companies' Transport and Rear H.Q. will be located near EBARTS FARM.

9. Battalion H.Q. will close at FOURDRINOY 1 p.m. 17th inst and open at WOOD S.E. MOLLIENS AU BOIS at time to be notified later.
H.Q. 58 Bn.M.G.C. will take over ~~from~~ H.Q. 47 Bn.M.G.C. at EBARTS FARM at 10.a.m. 20th inst.

10. ACKNOWLEDGE.

T.WATKINS. Captain and Adjt.

Copy No. 1. 58 Div G.
2. 58 Div A and Q.
3. A.Co.
4. B.Co.
5. C.Co.
6. D.Co.
7. 173 BDE.
8. 174 BDE.
9. 175 BDE.
10. 47 Bn.M.G.C.
11. C.O. 58 Bn.M.G.C.
12. 2nd in Command 58 Bn.
13. War Diary.
14 File.
15 and 16 Spare.

Appendix C.

SECRET. 58th BATTALION MACHINE GUN CORPS. Copy No. 7.

ORDER No.14.

Ref.Map. SHEET 62 D. 26th June 1918.

1. "A" Company, 58th Battalion, M.G.C. will be relieved in the line, in the Forward Left Sub-Sector, on the night June 27/28th by "C" Company, 58th Battalion M.G.C.
On relief "A" Company will march to EBART FARM, where they will take over billets and tentage vacated by "C" Company and will be the Company in Divisional Reserve.

2. All arrangements for relief will be made direct between Company Commanders concerned.

3. Receipts for stores handed over ~~to "C" Company~~ must be in this Office by 12 noon, 28th. Tentage receipts should be made out separately.

4. Relief complete will be reported by "A" Company on it's return to EBART FARM.

5. In future the reserve mobile section from the LAVIEVILLE LINE will be situated at S.E. corner of BOIS ROBERT, and the Section Officer will report his position to reserve Brigade H.Q., which will shortly be in Sunken Road, 100 yards South of this corner of the Wood.

6. The guns in Divisional Sector will in future be grouped under two Group Commanders as follows:-
LEFT SECTOR. Group Commander. O.C."A" Company.
Positions A.15, 17, 19, 7, 21, 22, 23.
Total 18 guns in position and mobile reserve section at Left Brigade H.Q.
RIGHT SECTOR. Group Commander. O.C."D" Company.
Positions A. 1, 24, 8, 6, 4, 25, 2.
Total 18 guns in position and mobile reserve section at Right Brigade H.Q.

7. Officers Commanding "A" and "D" Companies will arrange to take over their respective groups, as per above order, and on completion of handing over, O.C."B" Company will withdraw and establish his Company H.Q. in BOIS ROBERT.

8. All Administrative work of this Company will be carried on as before. Group Commanders will supervise and be responsible for the ordinary trench routine of the guns in LAVIEVILLE LINE now allotted to them, and for the arrangements of working parties, harrassing fire and other tasks, which the guns may be called upon to carry out.

9. ACKNOWLEDGE.

R.M.BLOMFIELD 2nd Lieut
and A/Adjt.

Copy No. 1. "A" Co.
2. "B" Co.
3. "C" Co.
4. "D" Co.
5. O.C.58 Bn. M.G.C
6. 2nd in Command 58th Bn.M.G.C.
7. War Diary.
8. File.

War Diary

Instructions regarding War Diaries and Intelligence Summaries are contained in F. S. Regs., Par. II. and the Staff Manual respectively. Title pages will be prepared in manuscript.

HEADQUARTERS, 58TH BATTALION, M.G. CORPS. No. A1239 Date.........

WAR DIARY
or
~~INTELLIGENCE SUMMARY.~~
(*Erase heading not required.*)

58th Battalion Machine Gun Corps July 1st – 31st

Army Form C. 2118.

VS 5

Place	Date	Hour	Summary of Events and Information	Remarks and references to Appendices
EBARTS FARM	1st		B C, D Coys in the line. A Coy in Reserve carried out training. Barrages were fired in conjunction with minor operations carried out on our Right. 2nd Lt RAS McDonald joined from the 29th Batt. M.G.C. and was evacuated. (accidental injury) 4 OR evacuated.	62° C1c
	2nd		B. C. D Coys in the line A Coy in Reserve carried out training. Harassing fire was carried out at night. 2 OR rejoined from Hospital. 2 OR evacuated.	
	3rd		B C. D Coys in the line A Coy in Reserve carried out training. On the night of the 3/4th a 'Chinese attack' was carried out and barrages were fired in conjunction with minor operations carried out on our left. 1 OR evacuated.	
	4th		B. C. D Coys in the line. A Coy in Reserve carried out training.	
	5th		A Coy relieved B Coy in the LAVIEVILLE Line with their Coy HQ in BOIS ROBERT	– C11c
			B Coy relieved D Coy in the right sector. D Coy marched to EBARTS FARM in Div. Reserve	– C1c
	5th		LIEUT H. USHER MC and 2nd Lt T D HAMPTON joined from Base.	
	6th		AB & C Coys in the line. D Coy in Reserve carried out training	
	7th		AB + C Coys in the line. D Coy in Reserve carried out training. Harassing fire was carried out during night 7/8th. 2 ORs rejoined from Hospital	
	8th		AB + C Coys in the line. D Coy in Reserve carried out training. Practice manning battle stations	

A6945 Wt. W11422/M1160 35,000 12/16 D. D. & L. Forms/C./2118/14.

Instructions regarding War Diaries and Intelligence Summaries are contained in F. S. Regs., Par. II. and the Staff Manual respectively. Title pages will be prepared in manuscript.

HEADQUARTERS 59TH BATTALION, M.G. CORPS.
No. ....
Date ....

WAR DIARY
or
~~INTELLIGENCE SUMMARY.~~
(*Erase heading not required.*)

Army Form C. 2118.

58 Battalion
Machine Gun Corps
July 1st – 31st

Place	Date	Hour	Summary of Events and Information	Remarks and references to Appendices
EBARTS FARM	8th		stations at 8.30 p.m. D Coy (in reserve) marched to C 20 d 10 15 and reported to Advanced	62 D C 1c
			Bde HQ. C 14 c by 11 pm. 12.20 A.M. Normal dispositions resumed. Harassing fire	
			was carried out during night 8/9th. 1 O R rejoined from Hospl.	
	9th		A B + C Coys in the line. D coy in reserve carried out training. Harassing fire	
			was carried out during night 9/10th. 3200 rounds were fired in Test Barrage on S.O.S line	
			of left Group. Battery + Infy Company Commanders convinced of safety of ~~[illegible]~~ own troops	
			1 O.R. evacuated 1 O R rejoined from hospl.	
	10th		A B + C Coys in the line. D Coy in reserve carried out training. Harassing	
			fire was carried out during night 10/11. 1 O.R. left for U.K. for Commission.	
	11th		A B + C Coys in the line, D Coy in reserve carried out training. Harassing 1 O.R. reinforcement.	
			fire was carried out during night 11/12.	
	12th		A B + C Coys in the line. D Coy in reserve carried out training. Harassing	
			fire was carried out during night 12/13th. The first of a series of Refresher Courses	
			under Battn Orders was commenced, under Lt BANKS. 1 officer + 4 o.r's per company attended. 12 O R [illegible]	
	13th		A B + C Coys in line. On night 13/14 D Coy relieved A in ~~[illegible]~~ LAVIEVILLE LINE. A Coy relieved	62 D D 11
			B Coy in the Right Sub Sector forward positions. B coy marched back to EBARTS FARM, in	62 D C 1c

A6945 Wt. W11422/M1160 350,000 12/16 D. D. & L. Forms/C./2118/14.

Instructions regarding War Diaries and Intelligence Summaries are contained in F. S. Regs., Part II. and the Staff Manual respectively. Title pages will be prepared in manuscript.

HEADQUARTERS, 58TH BATTALION, M.G. CORPS.

WAR DIARY
or
~~INTELLIGENCE~~ SUMMARY.
(Erase heading not required.)

58th Battalion Machine Gun Corps
July 1st – 31st

Army Form C. 2118.

Place	Date	Hour	Summary of Events and Information	Remarks and references to Appendices
EBARTS FARM	13		in Divl Reserve. Harassing fire was carried out during the night. R.S.M. returned to Base.	62 D C/c
	14		A. C + D coys in the line. B Coy in reserve attended church parade. Harassing fire was carried out during the night. During the day a gun at E.13b was hit but immediately replaced by gun from mobile section & the damaged gun was repaired by Company Artificer.	
	15		A C + D Coys in the line. B in reserve carried out training. Harassing fire was carried out during the night. 1 O.R. reported from Base.	
	16		A C + D Coys in the line B Coy in reserve carried out training. Harassing fire was carried out during the night. 6 O.R's evacuated	
	17		A C & D Coys in the line B Coy in reserve carried out training. Harassing fire was carried out during the night. Two Coys of the 124th American M.G. Battn were attached to this Bn for instruction in the line, for a period of 48 hours. Personnel only went into the line but the men of the ~~the~~ American M.G. Battn showed great keenness & desire to learn all about line work from our gun numbers. The officers were attached to the various Battery H.Qs & also were very keen to learn the duties of a Battery Commander in the line. 2 O.R's rejoined from Hospital. 3 O.R's evacuated. Capt E.J. Dooley evacuated.	

A6945 Wt W1422/M1160 350,000 12/16 D. D. & L. Forms/C/2118/14.

HEADQUARTERS.
58TH BATTALION.
M.G. CORPS.

Instructions regarding War Diaries and Intelligence Summaries are contained in F. S. Regs., Part II. and the Staff Manual respectively. Title pages will be prepared in manuscript.

WAR DIARY
or
~~INTELLIGENCE SUMMARY.~~
(*Erase heading not required.*)

Army Form C. 2118.

58th Battalion
Machine Gun Corps
July 1st – 31st

Place	Date	Hour	Summary of Events and Information	Remarks and references to Appendices
EBARTS FARM	18th		A C + D Coys in the line. B Coy in reserve carried out training. Americans attached had experience in assisting with the harassing fire that was carried out during the night. The 2nd Battn Refresher course assembled. 1 OR evacuated 1 OR rejoined from hospl	62D C.1.c
	19th		A C + D Coys in the line. B Coy in reserve carried out training. Americans came out of the line. Harassing fire was carried out during the night. 2 ORs evacuated. 2 ORs rejoined from hospl. Lt S.H. Hills from Base.	
	20th		A C + D Coys in the line. B Coy in reserve carried out training. Harassing fire was carried out during the night. 1 OR rejoined from Hospital.	
	21st		B Coy relieved D Coy in the ~~[illegible]~~ LAVIEVILLE System. D Coy relieved C Coy in the left forward sector. C Coy marched back to EBARTS FARM in Divisional Reserve. 1 OR evacuated	62D D.1.b 62D C.1.c
	2[illegible]		The remainder of the two companies C + D of the 124th American Battn. approx 3 officers + 95 ors to each company were attached to the left + right forward coys A + D Coys respectively, for a 48 hour tour of instruction in the line. Every possible chance of picking up valuable knowledge was given to the Americans on the night of going into the line as our C + D coys were also relieving, so that they experienced a proper relief. Transport of the American Battn was also used for taking the rations up to the line.	

A6945 Wt. W11422/M1160 350,000 12/16 D. D. & L. Forms/C./2118/14.

Instructions regarding War Diaries and Intelligence Summaries are contained in F. S. Regs., Part II. and the Staff Manual respectively. Title Pages will be prepared in manuscript.

WAR DIARY or ~~INTELLIGENCE~~ SUMMARY

(Erase heading not required.)

Army Form C. 2118.

58th Bn Machine Gun Corps
July 1st - 31st 1918

Place	Date	Hour	Summary of Events and Information	Remarks and references to Appendices
EBARTS FM	21		A gas projector attack was carried out on the enemy's lines together with a Stokes mortar bombardment of gas & smoke shells. Our machine guns cooperated with the artillery in harassing the tracks in the vicinity of the area which was bombarded.	62 D O.C
	22		A B + D Coys in the line. C in reserve bathed & cleaned up kit etc after coming out of the line. Harassing fire was carried out during the night. C + D Coys of the 124th American M G Battn in the line with our A + D Coys assisted in carrying out the above fire. 3 OR from Base 1 OR evacuated.	
	23		A B + D Coys in the line. C in reserve carried out training. Harassing fire was carried out during the night. A 15 Batty fired on its S.O.S line at 10.55 p.m in response to a call from Bde. Rds fired + 500.	
	24		A B + D Coys in the line. C in reserve carried out training. Harassing fire was carried out during the night. The two companies of 124 American Bn came out of the line. 2 OR's reported from Base and 1 from hospital. 2 OR evacuated. Lt + Or 1 Abrams reported from Infantry Base.	
	25		A B + D Coys in the line. C in reserve carried out training. In conjunction with a raid at 10.AM by the 8th Bn London Regt on enemy front system from E 1269.0 to E 8 c 8035 including the Quarry in E 14 c 2575 + the Hook in E 8 c, Our guns cooperated with the Artillery in putting down barrages as follows:- E 8 b 21 - E 8 c 9.9, E 8 b 82 - E 9 c 9.8, E 13 d 46 - E 14 0 11, E 20 a 39 to E 20 a 96. Total rounds fired 31000. Seventeen prisoners were captured by the raiding party. Harassing fire was carried out during the night. 1 OR reported from Hospital. 1 OR to 56 Div Signals.	62 D
	26		A B + D Coys in the line. C in reserve carried out training. Harassing fire was carried out during the night. C Coys 124th American M G Bn took over	

20

2449 Wt. W14957/M90 750,000 1/16 J.B.C. & A. Forms/C.2118/12.

Army Form C. 2118.

Instructions regarding War Diaries and Intelligence Summaries are contained in F. S. Regs., Part II. and the Staff Manual respectively. Title Pages will be prepared in manuscript.

HEADQUARTERS, 58TH BATTALION, M.G. CORPS.

WAR DIARY
or
~~INTELLIGENCE SUMMARY~~

(Erase heading not required.)

58 Bn Machine Gun Corps

July 1st – 31st 1918

Place	Date	Hour	Summary of Events and Information	Remarks and references to Appendices
EBARTS FARM	26		20 gun positions in the sector. The six guns of A Coy which were relieved were then located in vicinity of FRANVILLERS. Also the 47th M.G. Bn took over the remaining gun positions in the left forward sector from D Coy which afterwards marched to FRANVILLERS into billets. The 2nd Life Gds M G Bn took over the remaining gun positions of B Coy in the reserve line, B Coy then marching back to BOIS ROBERT. Harassing fire was carried out during the night.	62D C1C 62D C29a – C29a – C11c
	27	⇒	A Coy (less 6 guns) in the line D Coy in billets at Franvillers. B Coy relieved the 8th Australian Bde M. Guns taking over 12 positions north of the River ANCRE 'C' Coy in reserve carried out training. Harassing fire was carried out during the night by A Coy assisted by American Machine Gunners.	
	28	⇒	A + B Coys in the line D Coy in billets at FRANVILLERS. C Coy in reserve attended church parade. In conjunction with a minor operation carried out by the 5th Australian Division our machine guns cooperated with the Artillery in two Chinese Attacks in all 16 guns firing. Those guns under the Americans which fired were superintended by our Officers. Total number of rounds fired 24000.	–
	29		A + B coys in the line. C Coy in reserve carried out training. D Coy took over 10 positions from the 8th Australian Bde M. Gunners.	

2449 Wt. W14957/M90 750,000 1/16 J.B.C. & A. Forms/C.2118/12.

Instructions regarding War Diaries and Intelligence Summaries are contained in F. S. Regs., Part II. and the Staff Manual respectively. Title Pages will be prepared in manuscript.

HEADQUARTERS, 58TH BATTALION, M.G. CORPS.
No. ......
Date ......

WAR DIARY
or
INTELLIGENCE SUMMARY

(Erase heading not required.)

Army Form C. 2118.

58 Bn Machine Gun Corps
July 1st – 31st 1918

Place	Date	Hour	Summary of Events and Information	Remarks and references to Appendices
EBARTS FARM	29		~~from~~ Harassing fire was carried out during the night.	62 D C.10
	30		B & D Companies in the line. C Company relieved A Company in the left Brigade Sector ~~–~~ taking over the positions held conjointly by A Company & the 124th M.G. Bn Americans. B Coy took over A, position from A Coy (D 2 4 d 4 8). 2nd Life Guards M.G. Coy attached to this Battalion took over 8 gun positions in the reserve line of the left Brigade Sector. On the completion of the reliefs the line was held as follows:-	
			C Coy (left) 12 guns in position 4 in reserve	
			B " (centre) 12 " " " 4 " "	
			D " (right) 11 " " " 5 " "	
			2nd Life Guards M.G. Bn 8 guns in position.	
			Harassing fire was carried out during the night by all companies.	
	31		B.C. & D Coys in the line. A in reserve carried out training. Harassing fire was carried out during the night. 7 ORs evacuated. 1 OR rejoined from Hospital	

2449 Wt. W14957/M90 750,000 1/16 J.B.C. & A. Forms/C.2118/12.

SECRET. **58th BATTALION MACHINE GUN CORPS.** Copy No. 5

ORDER No.16.

Ref.Map. Sheet SENLIS 1:20000. July 16th 1918.

1. The 174th INFANTRY BRIGADE will carry out a raid on enemy trenches as shown on attached map at a date and hour to be notified later.

2. Machine Guns will cooperate by firing the following barrages, on the flank of the attack, as shown on map attached.

3. TARGET REFERENCES.

X Battery (4 guns) on X, Target E 8 b. 8.2. to E 9 c.95.75.
A17 " (2 ") " S.O.S. Lines E 8 b. 2.1. to E 8 d. 9.8.
A6 " (2 ") " S.O.S. " E 20 a. 4.8. to E 20 a.9.7.
A19 " (2 ") " E 13 d. 4.6. - E 14 c.1.1.

Total 10 Guns.

RATES OF FIRE.

Zero to Zero plus 8	Rapid.
Zero plus 8 to Zero plus 30	100 rounds per minute.
Zero plus 30 15 Zero plus 50	Slow.

4. The signal for withdrawal will be a rifle grenade bursting into three stars Red over Red over Red, and will be fired under Battalion arrangements at Zero plus 30 unless in the opinion of the Battalion Commander it should be fired earlier. Should the latter occur Batteries will still carry out the same programme as above.

5. Under no circumstances will any reference to this operation be made in conversation on the telephone forward of Reserve Brigade Headquarters.

6. Right Group Commander will arrange to withdraw on the morning of the raid the guns and teams from A 10 position leaving one sentry at each emplacement.
These guns will occupy the old emplacements at A 8 and be in a position there by 12.15 a.m. ZERO day.
They will return to A 10 position on completion of the raid and when the trenches are clear at the discretion of Officer in command.

T.WATKINS Captain & Adjt.

Copy No 1. 58th Division "G"
2. 174 Infantry Brigade.
3. Left Group Commander.
4. Right Group Commander.
5. War Diary.
6. File.

SECRET. 58th BATTALION, MACHINE GUN CORPS. Copy No....4..

Amendment to Order No. 16, dated July 16th 1918.

Ref. Map, Sht SENLIS, 1/20,000. July 23rd 1918.

1. The Raid will be carried out at 10.a.m. on the 25th July, 1918, by the 8th London Regiment.

2. Para 6 will be cancelled, and the guns and teams will remain at "A 16" Battery Position.

3. Watches will be synchronized at Right Brigade Headquarters, D.21.b.5.1. at 7.a.m. on the 25th July.

4. ACKNOWLEDGE.

T. WATKINS, Capt & Adjt.

Distribution.

1. O.C. 58th Bn M.G.C.
2. Left Group Commander.
3. Right Group Commander.
4. War Diary.
5. File.

SECRET. **58th BATTALION MACHINE GUN CORPS.** COPY NO...7..

SPECIAL ORDER.

Ref. Map. Sheet SENLIS 1/20,000. 20th July 1918.

1. The remainder of C & D Companies, 124th M.G. Battn. American Army will be attached to A & D Companies respectively of this Battn. for a 48 hour tour of instruction in the line, from 21/22nd to 22/23rd inst.
Each American Company will have 2 or 3 Officers and about 96 other ranks.

2. C & D Companies American Battn. will meet guides of A & D Companies respectively at BAIZIEUX CHATEAU at 7.30.p.m. night 21/22nd inst.
Ration Limbers of A & D Companies of this Battn. will collect rations of C & D Companies American Battn. respectively at BAZIEUX CHATEAU at same time, conveying them to their respective Company H.Qs.

3. Each American Company will be divided so that there will be an equal number of N.C.Os. and men for each Battery.
Officers will be accomodated as in the previous tour.

4. Guides for each Battery position and Section H.Q. will be at each Company H.Q. at a convenient time.

5. Every effort must be made to give as much guidance and instruction as possible.
The American Machine Gunners should have an opportunity to fire the guns engaged in Harassing Fire.

6. ACKNOWLEDGE.

Distribution.
1. "A" Company. 58th Bn. M.G.C.
2. "B" " " " "
3. "C" " " " "
4. "D" " " " "
5. 58th Div. "G" (for information)
6. 124th M.G. Bn. American Army.
7. War Diary.
8. File.

T. WATKINS. Capt & Adjt.

SECRET. 58th BATTALION MACHINE GUN CORPS. COPY NO. 12.

Order No. 17.

Ref Map, Sheet SENLIS 1/20,000. 24th July 1918.

1. Two Companies of the 124th American M.G. Battalion, each Company having a strength of ten guns, will take over positions in the forward area of the Divisional Sector on the night of 26/27th inst.

2. At the end of the period i.e. on night 30/31st inst they will be relieved by the same sections of the 58th Battalion.

3. "C" Company, 124th American M.G. Bn. will ~~xxxx~~ be in the RIGHT Brigade Sector.
"D" Company, 124th American M.G. Bn. will be in the LEFT Brigade Sector.

4. To carry out this relief 2 Sections of "D" Company, 58th Bn. M.G.C. and 2 Sections "A" Coy. 58th Bn. M.G.C. will be withdrawn from the line and will be located temporarily in BOIS ROBERT.
Tentage being arranged from respective Companies' Rear H.Q.

5. Gun Positions in completion of relief will be occupied as follows:-

RIGHT Brigade Sector.

A 1. 2 guns, 58th Battn.
A 6 (2 guns, 58th Battn.
(2 guns, 124th American Bn. M.G.C.
A24. 2 guns, 124th American Bn. M.G.C.
A30. 2 guns, " " " "
A10 2 guns, " " " "
A 2. 2 guns, " " " "

LEFT Brigade Sector.

A 7(2 guns, 58th Battn. M.G.C.
(2 guns, 124th American Bn. M.G.C.
A19(2 guns, 58th Battn. M.G.C.
(2 guns, 124th American Bn. M.G.C.
A17 2 guns, 124th American Bn. M.G.C.
A20 2 guns, " " " "
A15 2 guns, " " " "

"D" Company 124th American Battn. M.G.C.

All other gun positions not mentioned above will be manned as at present.

6. In the event of the order "Man Battle Stations" being received, the 4 Sections of 58th Battn. will take up positions in the FRANVILLERS Switch and VILLA Front Sector C.17.a. & b. and these positions will be reconnoitred by Company and Section Officers by mid-day 27th inst.

7. The following articles will be handed over as trench stores and mutual arrangements will be made between Company Commanders to exchange or recover on completion of the tour such articles as may be necessary.

"T" base platforms
Camouflage.
Range Boards.
Ten Belt Boxes per gun.
Condensor Petrol Tins.
Zero Posts.
Reserve Rations.
Sandbags.
Tools.
All Fire Order and Gun)
S.A.A. Position Orders)
Supply of Maps.
"T" Aiming Posts.
Reserve Water.

Receipts must be made out carefully beforehand, separate receipts being made as follows:-
(1) Reserve Rations and Water.
(2) S.A.A. and Hand Grenades.
(3) All other material.

8. The following Officers and N.C.Os. in each Sector will remain for 24 hours after relief or longer if required.

   1 Company Commander or 2nd in Command of Company.
   1 Officer per Section.
   1 N.C.O. per sub-section.

9. Captain Walker "B" Company, 58th Battalion will arrange accomodation for the Transport of the 124th American Bn. M.G.C, either in BAZIEUX or BOIS ROBERT.

10. Location of H. Qrs of the 124th American Bn. M.G.C. will be notified later.

11. Supplies will be sent forward in the same manner as at present and Company and Section Officers will be careful to point out to the relieving unit the best route for limbers and the nearest point to their posts at which rations may be dumped.

12. Guides and other minor points concerning the relief, will be arranged mutually betweenCompany Commanders.

13. Signal and Telephonic communications will remain as at present under Command of Signalling Officer, 58th Battalion.

14. The Mobile Sections in Brigade Reserve will be found as at present by 58th Battalion.

T. WATKINS Capt & Adjt.

Distribution.
1. 58th Division "G".
2. 124th American Bn. M.G.C.
3. " " " "
4. 173rd Inf. Brigade
5. 174th " "
6. 175th " "
7. "A" Company, 58th Bn.
8. "B" " " "
9. "C" " " "
10. "D" " " "
11. O.C. 58th Bn.
12. War Diary.
13. File.

SECRET. **58th BATTALION MACHINE GUN CORPS.** COPY NO. 12.

ORDER NO. 19.

26th July 19[illegible].

1. "C" & "D" Companies will relieve the 8th Australian Brigade Machine Guns in the line on the night 27/28th inst. and 29/30th inst. respectively.

2. "C" Company will take over the 10 gun positions South of the River ANCRE.
"D" Company will take over 10 gun positions North of the River ANCRE.

3. Company and Section Commanders will get in touch with the Australian Machine Gun Bn. and thoroughly reconnoitre their Sectors.

4. All arrangements for guides and reliefs will be made between Companies concerned.

5. It will be necessary to concentrate the guns in pairs or Sections as soon as possible. Company Commanders will therefore render a report to this office with their suggestions by 10.a.m. 28th inst.

6. O.C. Signals will arrange the necessary alterations in the telephonic communications.

7. The location of Company H.Q. and Reserve Sections will be notified to this office when decided upon.

8. Code word for this relief will be "[illegible]".

9. ACKNOWLEDGE.

T. WATKINS. Capt & Adjt.

Distribution.
1. 58th Division. "G"
2. 173rd Inf. Bde.
3. 174th " "
4. 175th " "
5. O.C."A" Coy. 58th Bn.
6. O.C."B" Coy. " "
7. O.C. "C" Coy. " "
8. O.C."D" Coy. " "
11. Signal Officer, 58th Bn.
10. C.O. 58th Bn.
9. 8th Australian M.G. Bn.
12. War Diary.
13. File.

SECRET. 58th BATTALION MACHINE GUN CORPS. COPY NO....

ORDER NO. 18.

Ref Map. Sheet SENLIS 1/20,000. 25th July 1918.

1. Owing to the redistribution of the Divisional Sector, it is necessary to cancel Order No. 17., paras. 2.3.4.5. & 6.

2. Gun positions to be taken over by 124th American M.G. Bn. will now be as under, on night 26/27th.

"C" Company, 124th American M.G. Bn.
A 24, 2 guns.
A 2, 4 "
A 25, 2 guns, with 2 guns of "A" Company 58th Battn.
A 4, 2 "

"D" Company, 124th American M.G. Bn.
A 6, 4 guns,
A 7, 2 guns with 2 guns of "A" Company 58th Battn.
A 30, 2 "
A 10, 2 "

3. "A" Company, 58th Bn. will take over 2 gun positions in A 25 and 2 gun positions in A 7.
In each of these 2 positions there will therefore be:-
2 guns 124th American M.G. Bn.
2 " 58th Bn. M.G.C.
"A" Company will also have 2 guns remaining in A 1 position.

4. O.C. "A" Company, 58th Bn. will make all arrangements for handing over the positions to the 124th American M.G. Bn. and will remain at his present Company H.Q. until further orders.

5. Guides from each Gun position will meet the 124th American M.G. Bn. on the ALBERT-AMIENS Road at CROSS ROADS D.21.a.6.7.
"C" Company, 124th American M.G. Bn. arriving there at 8.30.p.m. and "D" Company 124th American M.G. Bn. at 9.30.p.m.
All further relief arrangements to be made direct between O.C. "A" Company, 58th Bn. and Company Commanders, 124th American M.G. Bn.

6. Group Commanders will arrange to accomodate 4 guns in the positions at present held by 2 guns only, namely:- A 6. A 7. and A 2.

7. Section Officers must understand that they will not in all cases relieve the American Battn. at the end of their 4 days tour of duty and therefore any articles they hand over, such as Range Boards, "T" base platforms, etc must be only if they are surplus to their requirements. The 10 Belt Boxes must be in exchange.

8. On the same night 26/27th, the 47th Bn. M.G.C. will take over the following positions:- A 29. A 15. A 17. A 19.
and the 2nd Life Guards Machine Gun Bn.:- A 20. A 21. A 22. A 23.

9. On completion of these reliefs Companies will be disposed as follows:-
"A" Company, 6 guns in position. A 1. A 25. A 7.
4 " Brigade Mobile Reserve.
6 " to be located in vicinity of FRANVILLERS.
"B" Company, in bivouac in BOIS ROBERT.
"D" Company, in bivouac or billets in FRANVILLERS.
"C" Company, ESBART FARM.

10. The reserve rations and ammunition in positions taken over by the 47th M.G. Bn. and 2nd Life Guards M.G. Bn. will be handed over and the usual receipts obtained.

11. O.C. "A" Company, will arrange to carry on the working party required by Tunnelling Coy. at A 10 position.

12. The following code-words will be wired to Battn. H.Q. when reliefs are complete.

Relief by	2nd Life Guards M.G. Bn.	GUERNSEY.
" "	47th Bn. M.G.C.	PORTLAND.
" "	124th American M.G. Bn.	~~[illegible]~~ PUTNEY.

13. ACKNOWLEDGE.

T. WATKINS. Capt. & Adjt.

Distribution.

1. 58th Division "G"
2. 2nd Life Gds. M.G. Regt.
3. 47th M.G. Bn.
4. 124th American M.G. Bn.
5. 173rd Inf. Bde.
6. 174th " "
7. 175th " "
8. "A" Co. 58th Bn.
9. "B" Co. " "
10. "C" Co. " "
11. "D" Co. " "
12. O.C. 58th Bn.
13. War Diary.
14. File.

SECRET. 58th BATTALION MACHINE GUN CORPS. Copy No. 10

ORDER No.20.

Ref.Map. SENLIS 1/20000. 28th July 1918.

1. On the night July 28/29th the 5th AUSTRALIAN DIVISION on the right are carrying out a minor operation. ZERO hour will be notified later.

2. Machine Guns of 58th M.G.Bn and 47th M.G.Bn. will cooperate in two "Chinese" attacks at ZERO and ZERO plus 54 minutes by firing on normal S.O.S. lines as follows:-

Battery.	Time.	Rate of fire.
A 2.	Z to Z plus 5.	250 rounds per minute.
A 7. (4 guns)	Z plus 5 to Z plus 15.	125 rounds per minute.
A 17.	Z plus 54 to Z plus 70.	125 rounds per minute.
A 30.	do.	do.
A 24.	do.	do.
A 1.	do.	do.

In addition 4 guns of A 6 Battery will fire on QUARRY in E 14 c.

Z to Z plus 5.	250 rounds per minute.
Z plus 5 to Z plus 15.	125 rounds per minute.

3. O.C."A" Company 58th Bn.M.G.C. will arrange to have an Officer to superintend the firing at each Battery position in his Sector.

4. Watches will be synchronised by telephone at 9.15.p.m. July 28th 1918.

5. ACKNOWLEDGE.

Distribution.

1. O.C."A" Co. 58 Bn.M.G.C.
2. 47th Bn.M.G.Corps
3. 124th A.M.G.Bn.
4. 58th Div. "G" (For information)
5. 58th Div. Artillery. "
6. 173.Inf.Bde. "
7. 174.Inf.Bde. "
8. 175.Inf.Bde. "
9. O.C.58th Bn.M.G.C.
10. War Diary
11. File.

T.WATKINS Captain & Adjt.

SECRET. 58th BATTALION MACHINE GUN CORPS. COPY NO. 15.

ORDER NO. 21.

Ref Map. Sheet 62 d.N.E. 1/20,000. 29th July 1918.

1. "C" Company, 58th Bn. will relieve "A" Company in the Left Brigade Sector on night 30/31st inst, taking over positions at present held conjointly by "A" Company, 58th Bn. and the 124th American M.G. Bn.

2. "B" & "D" Companies 58th Bn. will on the same night, rearrange their guns to conform with the positions mentioned in para 4.

3. The Company 2nd Life Guards M.G. Regt at present attached to 58th Division will take over with one Section the position A 25 also place two guns in position at D.16.b.1.1. and two guns at D.22.b.40.35.

4. On completion of reliefs positions will then be occupied as follows:-

"C" Coy. 58th Bn.
A.10. A 30. A 7. A 4. A 2. A 24. - 2 guns at each position.
Total 12 guns.

"B" Coy. 58th Bn.
A 1 in addition to the Australian positions taken over on 27/28th inst. They will vacate gun position No. 6 and hand over gun position No. 7 (Australian Nos) to "D" Company. Total 12 guns

"D" Coy. 58th Bn.
Will hold the 10 gun positions taken over from the Australians South of the River and in addition the position numbered 7 in D.30.b.2.1. at present held by "B" Company. - Total 11 guns.

2nd Life Guards M.G. Regt.
A 25 position - 4 guns.
D.16.b.1.1. - 2 "
D.22.b.40.35. - 2 " Total 8 guns.

5. Sections of 58th Bn. in reserve will be:-

"C" Company (Major Drew) 4 guns, LEFT Brigade.
"D" " (Capt.Emslie) 5 " RIGHT Brigade.
"B" " (Capt. Walker) 4 " Divisional Reserve.

6. "A" Company on relief will withdraw to ESBART FARM.

7. Three separate receipts will be rendered in duplicate as follows:-
(1) Reserve Rations and Water.
(2) S.A.A. & Grenades.
(3) Trench Stores.
and forward to Battalion Headquarters by mid-day 31st inst.

8. 2 guns 47th Bn. M.G.C. will occupy position at A 6.

9. Relief complete will be wired by Codeword "STRIKE".

10. ACKNOWLEDGE.

T. WATKINS. Capt & Adjt.

Distribution.
1. 58th Division "G"
2. O.C."A" Co.58thBn.
3. O.C. "B"" "
4. O.C."C" " "
5. O.C."D" " "
6. 173rd Inf.Bde.
7. 174th " "
8. 175th " "
9. 47th Bn. M.G.C.
10. 124th American M.G.Bn.
11. 2nd Life Gds.M.G.Regt.
12. 5th Aust. M.G.Bn.
13. C.O. 58th Bn.
14. S.O. " "
15. War Diary. ✓
16. File.

SECRET. **58th Battalion Machine Gun Corps.** Copy No. 1...

Order No. 22.

Ref Map Sheet 62D. N.E. 1/20,000. 31st July 1918.

1. On night 1/2nd August, 173rd Infantry Brigade will take over from 18th Division, the front as far South as where HAY STREET cuts the front line K.7.d.0.8.

2. Reserve Section of "D" Company will occupy four gun positions at the following locations:-

   1 Gun K.7.a.75.15.
   1 Gun J.12.b.55.85.
   1 Gun J.12.a.75.95.
   1 Gun J.12.a.5.8.

3. O.C. "D" Company will get into touch with the Commander, Left Company, 18th Battalion M.G.C. at J.10.d.9.4. making all necessary arrangements for the relief.

4. Relief complete will be wired by codeword "EMSLIE".

5. ACKNOWLEDGE.

T. WATKINS Capt & Adjt.

Distribution.
1. 58th Division "G" (for information)
2. 173rd Inf. Bde. " "
3. O.C. 58th Bn.
4. O.C. "D" Coy. 58th Bn.
5. War Diary.
6. File.

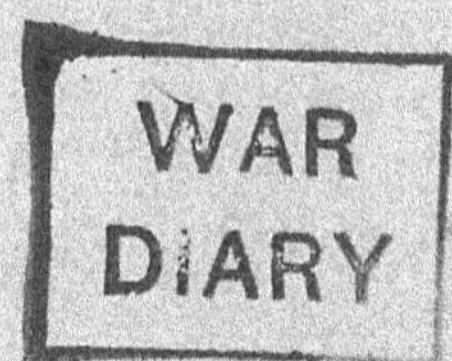

58th BATTALION, MACHINE GUN CORPS.

A P R I L

1 9 1 8

Instructions regarding War Diaries and Intelligence Summaries are contained in F. S. Regs., Part II. and the Staff Manual respectively. Title pages will be prepared in manuscript.

~~WAR DIARY~~ or ~~INTELLIGENCE SUMMARY.~~
(Erase heading not required.)

[?] Battalion Machine Gun Corps.
April 1st to 30th 1918.

Vol. 2

Place	Date	Hour	Summary of Events and Information	Remarks and references to Appendices
BLERANCOURT	1st		Battalion H.Q at BLERANCOURT. A and D. Companies in training. No 3 Section of "B" Company relieved in Line on CANAL DEFENCE S.W. of BAC D'ARBLINCOURT. 3. Lewis Guns with teams withdrawn from BOURGUIGNON.	62 D.
	2nd		Battalion H.Q at BLERANCOURT closed at 12 midnight.	
		8.30 a.m	Under cover of mist an enemy raiding party, roughly 150 strong surprised Infantry Post in Southern end of AMIGNY-ROUY and captured one of "C" Company's Guns together with 4 other Ranks. 2nd Lieut R.A. ILLING organised a bombing party and reestablished the Post.	
			Four of "B" Co's guns attached to "C" Co. Remaining 3 Sections and Transport of "B" Co proceeded by road to LES CAVES.	
			Capt C.I. Morris "D" Co. admitted to Hospital and evacuated sick.	
			Capt E.G. Moore joined "D" Co for duty.	
	3rd	7.a.m	Battalion H.Q. and Transport moved by road to DOMMIERS.	
			A. Co moved by road to LE MESNIL.	
		7.45.a.m	B.Co. (less one Section) and Transport proceeded by road to DOMMIERS.	
		4.a.m	Relief of "B" Company's Section and one Section of "C" Company in Line by French complete.	
			Both Sections proceeded to PIERREMANDE.	
		6.p.m	" " Left for ARDIGNCOURT to join remainder of "C" Company.	
			D. Co moved to VASSENS.	
	4th		Battalion HQ closed at DOMMIERS and opened at GLISY. A Coy marched from LE MESNIL to AMBLENY.	
		5pm	B Coy (less one section) and Transport proceeded by road to entrain at VILLERS COTTERETS	
			C Coy left for COUTRY	
			D Coy proceeded to AMBLENY	

A5834 Wt. W4973/M687 750,000 8/16 D. D. & L. Ltd. Forms/C.2118/13

Instructions regarding War Diaries and Intelligence Summaries are contained in F. S. Regs., Part II. and the Staff Manual respectively. Title pages will be prepared in manuscript.

~~INTELLIGENCE SUMMARY.~~

(*Erase heading not required.*)

58 Battalion Machine Gun Corps

April 1st to 30th 1918.

Place	Date	Hour	Summary of Events and Information	Remarks and references to Appendices
GLISY	5th.		A Coy marched from AMBLENY, halted for a few hours at St PIERRE AIGLE and entrained at VILLERS COTTERETS	
		3am	B Coy (less one section) and Transport entrained for LONGEAU	
		11am	B Coy detrained and proceeded to GENTELLES. 10 Guns and teams took over positions in the line at U28d U9c.d and U10b. U11b.	
			C Coy entrained at VILLERS COTTERETS detrained at LONGEAU and encamped at N.30d.	
			D Coy left AMBLENY and marched to St PIERRE AIGLE.	
	6th		A Coy detrained at LONGEAU and proceeded to a spot in vicinity of BOIS de GENTELLES for defence of AMIENS	
			B Coy carried out harassing fire on enemy targets, 1500 rounds expended	
		6am	3 Sections of C Coy relieved ? M G Co. During relief enemy plane dropped two bombs on No 3. Section Casualties. two wounded	
		11am	D Coy entrained at VILLERS COTTERETS, detrained at LONGEAU 7th and marched to GLISY	
	7th		Enemy aircraft active, bombs dropped in vicinity of BOIS de GENTELLES	
			No 4 Section B Coy rejoined unit from 173 Infantry Brigade.	
	8th		2nd Lt R.A Isaac admitted to Hospital sick.	
			One section of A Coy detailed to fire Barrage - HANGARD (cancelled for 24 hours)	
			B Coy No 4 section proceeded to GLISY for instruction in Barrage work	
			One section of D Coy attached to B Coy for duty in the Line	
			4 Guns of D Coy sent into Line near HANGARD for Barrage work	
			4 Guns with teams under 2/Lt H.R. Westwood relieved 4 Guns of Australian Brigade near VILLERS BRETTONEUX.	
	9th		2/Lt J. Watkins appointed Adjutant to Battn vice Lieut CB Felton	
			Barrage section of A Coy withdrawn to GLISY to train in BARRAGE Drill.	

A5834 Wt. W4973/M687 750,000 8/16 D. D. & L. Ltd. Forms/C.2118/13

Instructions regarding War Diaries and Intelligence Summaries are contained in F. S. Regs., Part II. and the Staff Manual respectively. Title pages will be prepared in manuscript.

~~WAR DIARY~~ or INTELLIGENCE ~~SUMMARY.~~

(Erase heading not required.)

Machine Gun Corp.

April 1st to 30th 1918.

Place	Date	Hour	Summary of Events and Information	Remarks and references to Appendices
GLISY.	9th (contd)		3 Sections of B Coy with 10 Guns relieved by ? Australian Machine Gun Co.	
			8 Guns and teams with attached Section of D Coy took over new positions at U6 v1 and O3c Enemy heavily shelled B Coy's positions on night during day. 10,000 rounds fired on targets in P 27 d	
		3.30pm	1 Section of C Coy in reserve proceeded to GENTELLES for Barrage operations	
			4 Barrage Guns of D Coy withdrawn from line near HANGARD	
	10th		A Coy reconnoitred new positions in Right Sector of Reserve Line and 4 Guns moved into new positions.	
			B Coy HQ with Transport proceeded to GLISY. 8 Guns in line relieved and withdrawn to HQ to GLISY	
			One section of C Coy returned to GLISY for BARRAGE Drill	
	11th.			
	12th.		Enemy attack on HANGARD	
			9 officers reported for duty from Base Depot.	
	13th.		Barrage section of A Coy at GLISY rejoined Coy in Line Two section of D Coy attached to A Coy for duty. No 4 section B Coy rejoined unit	
			B Coy and Transport moved up to camp at O.26 d 7.0.	
			6 Guns of B coy relieved ? Australian ? in front of VILLERS BRETTONEUX. 4 Guns of B Coy relieved one section of A Coy at V27 d.	
			No 1 section C Coy rejoined Coy at N30 d.	
			No 2 — — — relieved by 4 Guns of B Coy in Reserve Line	
	14th.		Eight Gun positions in DOMART sector taken over from 18th Batn MGC by one section of A Coy and one section of D Coy. B Coy Transport proceeded to O.20 b 9 4 owing to heavy enemy shelling.	
			2 Guns of B Coy ordered to new position in U4 c.	

A5834 Wt. W4973/M687 750,000 8/16 D. D. & L. Ltd. Forms/C.2118/13

Instructions regarding War Diaries and Intelligence Summaries are contained in F. S. Regs., Part II. and the Staff Manual respectively. Title pages will be prepared in manuscript.

~~INTELLIGENCE SUMMARY.~~

(*Erase heading not required.*)

Machine Gun Coy

April 1st to 30th 1918.

Place	Date	Hour	Summary of Events and Information	Remarks and references to Appendices
FORT MANOIR FARM.	15th	12 noon	Batt. HQ closed at GLISY and opened at FORT MANOIR FARM (12 noon)	
			Position in DOMART sector inspected and fresh position occupied	
			Capt W.S. Ferrie reported from Base Depot and took over Command of D Coy.	
	16th		Enemy bombarded A Coy position in DOMART sector with 5.9s. B Coy carried out harassing fire on enemy targets in P.27 d. 2000 rounds fired.	
			2 sections of "C" Coy relieved by 8th Australian M.G. Coy and proceeded with Transport and Stores to GLISY	
			Capt. E.G. Moore. 5 Lon Regt ordered by Division to report 1/28 Battn London Regt	
	17th		A Coy No 15 Gun position in DOMART Sector received a direct hit and two of gun team killed.	
			Enemy bombarded DOMART VALLEY throughout night of 16/17th Large quantities of Gas shells caused a number of casualties. Positions for Indirect fire sited. B Coy fired 1500 rounds on enemy targets	
			2/Lt. H.J. Willen admitted to Hospital, sick, and evacuated.	
	18th		Batt. operation order No 4 sent out A Coy took over all Gun positions in DOMART Sector	
			4 Guns were withdrawn to the Coy HQ as Reserve.	
			No 1 Section of C Coy placed under orders of 36th Australian Infantry Bn (?).	
	19th		2/Lt R.A. Macdonald admitted to Hospital sick	
			A Coy 4 guns in Reserve took up prepared position	
		11pm	B Coy relieved by 8th Divisional M.G. Battn 3 Section of C Coy relieved 5th AM & Co taking over two Gun position in U22c area.	
			2 - - U7a -	
			~~4~~ - - U11a -	
			4 - - U9c cd.	
		7pm	4 Guns of D Coy under 2/Lt M.C. Perret and 2/Lt J Walton relieved A Coy team in support line.	
			4 Guns of D Coy ceased to be attached to A Coy and took up positions in support line.	

A5834 Wt. W4973/M687 750,000 8/16 D. D. & L. Ltd. Forms/C.2118/13

Instructions regarding War Diaries and Intelligence Summaries are contained in F. S. Regs., Part II. and the Staff Manual respectively. Title pages will be prepared in manuscript.

or

~~INTELLIGENCE SUMMARY.~~

(Erase heading not required.)

Machine Gun [illegible]

April 1st to 30th 1918.

Place	Date	Hour	Summary of Events and Information	Remarks and references to Appendices
GLISY	20th		A Coy carried out harassing fire	
			B Coy and Transport proceeded by road to BOUTILLERIE	
	21st		A Coy carried out harassing fire	
	22nd		A Coy carried out harassing fire	
			B Coy engaged in constructing model Machine Gun emplacements for inspection	
	23rd		A Coy carried out harassing fire	
			From information obtained from a prisoner an attack was to be made at 3am 24th but objectives	
			of attack and strength of enemy not known.	
		8.30pm	All guns visited and officers warned and S.O.S lines checked	
	24th	3.40am	Heavy enemy bombardment opened.	
		7am	Enemy attacked on 3 Division front from left of VILLERS BRETTONEAUX to right of HANGARD VILLAGE	
			and obtained local successes attack at U11a assisted by 2 Tanks S.O.S. was unobserved by mist	
			A Coys guns on SOS line immediately opened fire when news received that enemy were attacking	
			Two of A Coy Gun position Nos 15 & 16 received direct hits causing casualties to No 1 & 2 of each gun	
			Guns & RK were salved and alternative positions occupied	
			To conform with new Infantry line 3 guns Nos 3, 9 & 10 were moved to more tactical position	
			Enemy were engaged with direct fire in vicinity of HANGARD WOOD Nos 11 & 12 Guns received	
			direct hits and rendered useless 3 Guns of C Coy at U11a and two guns at U26b	
			captured all other guns held their ground. B Coy moved into Brigade Reserve in T9b	
			one section of B Coy proceeded to Batt HQ in Divisional Reserve	
			O.C B Coy reported completion of move to 175 Inf Brigade HQ and received orders to move	
			4 Guns into CACHY switch. N of GENTELLES and 4 Guns each to 9th & 12th Lon Regt holding Reserve Line.	
			S of GENTELLES	

A5834 Wt. W4973/M687 750,000 8/16 D. D. & L. Ltd. Forms/C.2118/13

Instructions regarding War Diaries and Intelligence Summaries are contained in F. S. Regs., Part II. and the Staff Manual respectively. Title pages will be prepared in manuscript.

~~INTELLIGENCE SUMMARY.~~

(Erase heading not required.)

Machine Gun Corps

April 1st to 30th 1918

Place	Date	Hour	Summary of Events and Information	Remarks and references to Appendices
GLISY	24th (Contd)		Move was completed by 11 am. Heavy shelling was in progress at the time, the enemy having attacked and driven in our front line S. of VILLERS BRETTONEAUX	
			Section reporting to 9th Battn took up position N & S of main road running through T.I.8.c	
			2 of Guns reporting to 12th Batt took up positions in Reserve Lines T.I.8.c. The other two guns being at disposal of Counter attack Coy. In spite of heavy hostile shelling, casualties in reaching Gun position were extremely light, one Gun and limber complete with team were destroyed by shell fire. Casualties in moving up 1 OR killed; 3 OR wounded.	
		3.40pm	Counter attack Coy of 9th Batt. moved forward to consolidate line running through U.9.	
			2 Guns under Lieut Wardle moved forward with the Coy. This officer was wounded and 2 OR killed on the way up, and a Sergeant took charge of the sub section and took up position in U.9.c	
		6.30pm	4 Guns N of GENTELLES ordered to take up Barrage position in U.9.a to assist in a Barrage in conjunction with an attack at 10 pm. Owing to a runner becoming a casualty the move was not completed before 2 am. Battery dug in at U.9.a.9.0.	
		10.30pm	Counter attack preceded by Artillery Bombardment practically reestablished line but situation at U16 and U17 still obscure.	
	25th		A Coy relieved by B Coy and withdrew to Co H.Q. at BOIS de GENTELLES. Prior to relief guns were returned to original positions.	
			B Coy 2 Guns in U.9.c received orders to withdraw and join 5 Guns already in position S. of GENTELLES.	
		12 noon	Orders sent to B. Coy. for these 7 guns to withdraw to Brigade Reserve in T.I.5.c. This was completed by 4 pm without casualties.	
		5 pm	B Coy with one section of D Coy attached ordered to relieve A Coy in DOMART Sector and prepare to fire a barrage to support an attack next morning. Major Mac Yack MC 2nd in Command of Batt. detailed to conduct barrage	

A5834 Wt. W4973/M687 750,000 8/16 D. D. & L. Ltd. Forms/C.2118/13

Instructions regarding War Diaries and Intelligence Summaries are contained in F. S. Regs., Part II. and the Staff Manual respectively. Title pages will be prepared in manuscript.

~~or INTELLIGENCE SUMMARY.~~

(*Erase heading not required.*)

Machine Gun Corps
April 1st to 30th 1918

Place	Date	Hour	Summary of Events and Information	Remarks and references to Appendices
GLISY	26th	2am	B. Coy. relief of A Coy completed casualties 3 OR wounded	
		5.15am	12 Guns of B Coy and 4 Guns of D Coy detailed for Barrage work under command of MAJOR M.W. TAIT MC opened fire as ordered. 30,000 rounds were expended. Enemy retaliation was extremely heavy. Casualties 1 OR Killed 2 OR wounded.	
		4.15pm	S.O.S. signal was sent up from HANGARD WOOD front. Guns opened fire and 23.000 rounds were fired between this time and 8pm. One gun was temporarily put out of action, repaired later.	
	27th	11pm.	B. Coy relieved by French and all Guns and material withdrawn. C Coy withdrew all Guns in line on completion of Infantry relief by French. 4 Guns of D Coy. relieved by French.	
	28th	4.30am	B. Coy. relief complete Casualties 2 OR wounded 1 OR Gassed Battn HQ. & Companies marched to AMIENS and embussed to YAUCOURT-BUSSUS	
YAUCOURT-BUSSUS.	29th		Companies Reorganising.	
	30th		Companies Reorganising	
			Total Casualties during April	
			Officers. Wounded 7. " (GAS) 5 Killed 1 Total 13	
			Other Ranks Killed 17. Wounded 110. " (accidental) 2. Missing 9. Died of Wounds 1. Total 139	

A5834 Wt. W4973/M687 750,000 8/16 D. D. & L. Ltd. Forms/C.2118/13

58th Divl. Troops

58th BATTALION

MACHINE GUN CORPS

A U G U S T 1 9 1 8

WAR DIARY
or
~~INTELLIGENCE SUMMARY.~~
(Erase heading not required.)

Army Form C. 2118.

Instructions regarding War Diaries and Intelligence Summaries are contained in F. S. Regs., Part II, and the Staff Manual respectively. Title pages will be prepared in manuscript.

58th Battalion Machine Gun Corps August 1st – 31st

Vol 6

Place	Date	Hour	Summary of Events and Information	Remarks and references to Appendices
EBARTS FARM	1		B C & D Coys in the line. A Coy in reserve carried out training. Harassing fire carried out during the night	62D.c.i.c
	2		B & D Coys in the line. A Coy moved by bus from EBARTS FM to HALLOY LES PERNOIS after being relieved by a coy of the 12th Batt M.G.C. 'C' Coy were relieved in the left sector by 12th Batt M.G.C. Transports of A & C Coys moved with 174 & 173 Brigade respectively to the new area. Indications that enemy is withdrawing from his front and support lines round ALBERT	Appendix [illegible]
	3	5am	C Coy embussed for PERNOIS. A Coy carried out training at HALLOY. B Coy in the line. D Coy relieved by D Coy 12th Batt M.G.C. & on relief marched to BEHENCOURT. B Coy relieved by A Coy 12th Batt M.G.C.	
	4		B Coy marched by road (with transport) to [illegible] in vicinity of VAUX sur SOMME. A Coy moved by bus transport by road to LA HOUSSOYE AREA and bivouaced in wood I.15 central. No 1 Sect C Coy attached to 174 Inf Brigade moved by bus transport by road to billets in LAHOUSSOYE remainder of Coy stayed at PERNOIS. D Coy in billets at BEHENCOURT	I.27.a, I.27.c

A6945 Wt. W11422/M1160 350,000 12/16 D. D. & L. Forms/C./2118/14.

Instructions regarding War Diaries and Intelligence Summaries are contained in F. S. Regs., Par. II. and the Staff Manual respectively. Title pages will be prepared in manuscript.

WAR DIARY
or
~~INTELLIGENCE SUMMARY.~~
(*Erase heading not required.*)

Army Form C. 2118.

58th Battalion
Machine Gun Corps
August 1st – 31st

Place	Date	Hour	Summary of Events and Information	Remarks and references to Appendices
PONT NOYELLES	4		H.Q closed at EBART FM on relief by 12th Batt MGC and opened at PONT NOYELLES	620 O18a
	5		A Coy preparing for line. B Coy erecting bivouacs in J27a-c. C Coy less 2 section at PERNOIS. No 1 sect at LAHOUSSOYE. No 4 sect embussed for PONT NOYELLES transport proceeded by road and reported to HQ 58th Batt MGC. D Coy carried out training at BEHENCOURT	
	6		A Coy moved from wood J15a to VAUX sur SOMME area. B Coy officers carried out a reconnaissance of the line in J19a and J21b but were interrupted by a hostile attack. 2 section relieve 2 sect of 18 Batt MGC in the SAILLY LE SEC area and the other 2 sections taking up position in J30c. C Coy 1 section at LAHOUSSOYE 1 sect at PONT NOYELLES remainder of Coy moved up from PERNOIS to PONT NOYELLES by road. D Coy carried out training	Appendix 1/2
		10pm	D Coy left for VAUX area	
	7		A Coy moved up at night to their assembly positions	
			B Coy preparing for line. Officers & NCOs carried out reconnaissance	
			C Coy No 1 Sect moved to valley by VAUX sur SOMME and at night moved into position at SAILLY LE SEC area. No 4 sect moved to valley by VAUX sur SOMME and at night moved to position in line	

A6945 Wt. W11422/M1160 350,000 12/16 D. D. & L. Forms/C./2118/14.

Army Form C. 2118.

Instructions regarding War Diaries and Intelligence Summaries are contained in F. S. Regs., Part II. and the Staff Manual respectively. Title pages will be prepared in manuscript.

WAR DIARY
or
~~INTELLIGENCE SUMMARY.~~
(Erase heading not required.)

58th Battalion
Machine Gun Corps
August 1st – 31st

Place	Date	Hour	Summary of Events and Information	Remarks and references to Appendices
PONT NOYELLES	7th		C Coy No 2 & 3 section moved to BOIS ESCARDONEUSE and bivouaced for the night	I 15a
			D Coy at VALLEY of VAUX sur SOMME preparing for line	I 7a
	8th – 13th		As per Appendix 3	Appendix 3
	14th		A and B Coys carried out training	
			C & D Coys bivouac in Key Wood	
	15th		A B C D Coys reorganising and carried out training	
			Major Drew and LIEUT DONOVAN proceeded to ENGLAND	
	16th		Coys carried out training	
KEY WOOD	17th	1000	Batt Headquarters closed at PONT NOYELLES opened at KEY WOOD	
			All Coys proceeded to Range near MIRVAUX for firing practice (8 guns per Coy)	T 22 d
			CAPT. W.J.N LITTLE joined from Base.	
	18th		All Coys carried out training. Church Parade	
	19th		All Coys carried out training	
	20th		Inspection of the Battalion by the G.O.C.	
	21st		All Coys carried out training } 21st – 31st see APPENDIX 4.	
	22nd		A + B Coys carried out training }	

C.P. Wilson Lieut-Col.
Cmdg. 58 Battalion M.G. Corps

D. D. & L., London, E.C.
(A7883) Wt. W803/M1672 350,000 4/17 Sch. 52a Forms/C/2118/14

SECRET.

Operations of the 58th Division from 8 - 13 August 1918.

MACHINE GUNS.

1. On August 3rd the first intimation was received of the forthcoming attack on the Fourth Army front, and of the extent and nature of the task allotted to the 58th Division in those operations. On that date 2 Companies of the M.G.Battalion were still in the line but were to be relieved that night; the other 2 Companies were in the back areas.

2. On August 5th, after conferences between the Brigade Commanders and the M.G.Battalion Commander on the previous day, instructions were issued as to the employment of the Machine Guns in the attack. These instructions are contained in Appendix 1. On these a map and further instructions were issued to the M.G.Commanders concerned giving the tasks etc. allotted to the various companies. These included covering fire for the advance.

3. As secrecy was an essential factor to the success of the operations the preparation of the emplacements etc. could not be undertaken until the night of August 7/8. But it was possible to select the positions which were on a forward slope during daylight and to reach the assembly positions during the night of August 6/7.

4. The task of constructing emplacements, getting up ammunition, guns, water etc.starting at dusk on the evening of the 7th and having everything ready to open fire at 4.20am the following morning reflects great credit on the units concerned. Added to which there was a certain amount of liveliness due to the attacks and counter attacks on this front during the two days preceeding the attack; and a good many casualties to personnel and animals occurred.

August 8th.

Zero hour on the morning of the 8th the attack started in a thick mist which instead of clearing became thicker as the morning advanced. All guns taking part in the initial barrage carried out their tasks as arranged and "B" Company went forward behind the 174th Infantry Brigade to previously selected localities in order to consolidate and prepare for a secondary barrage in support of the 173rd Infantry Brigade, the latter being rendered most difficult owing to the heavy mist.
Two sections of "D" Company (allotted the dual task of taking part in the secondary barrage and if necessary to cover any gap that might take place between ourselves and the left flank Division) went forward and took up positions to carry out the secondary barrage, no gap having taken place.
"A" Company, allotted the task of supporting and consolidating the gains of the 173rd Infantry Brigade worked forward in close touch with the Infantry affording them good covering fire, and taking up good defensive positions.
Later in the day 2 sections of "C" Company from Corps Reserve moved forward to augment the M.G. defence in view of an expected counter-attack from the N.E. In addition to this the 2 sections of "D" Company in Divisional Reserve were also ordered forward to a more central position N.W. of MALARD WOOD.
The section of "C" Company allotted the task of covering and supporting the attack on SAILLY LAURETTE having carried out this task proceeded about 7pm to perform a similar operation as regards the attack on CHIPILLY. For this purpose the Section Commander considerably intensified his covering fire by utilising 3 German Machine Guns in addition to his own.

August 9th.

At 5.30pm the 175th Infantry Brigade and the 131st American Regt. attacked in a N.E. direction. For this purpose "C" Company had been assembled in the early afternoon, their role being to consolidate in depth the gains of the 175th Infantry Bde. This was carried out successfully, 2 sections taking up positions in the trenches of the old AMIENS defences.

On the afternoon of the 9th "B" Company, 50th M.G.Bn. was placed under orders of O.C. 58th M.G.Battalion. On arrival these guns were ordered to take up positions astride the boundary line between the 58th Division and the 131st American Regt. The positions were occupied before dawn on the 10th and arrangements completed for a protective barrage.

August 10th.

The 2 sections of "D" Company in Divisional Reserve were also sent forward to provide the defence in depth and put down a protective barrage in front of our new line. The remaining 2 sections of "D" Company becoming local reserve at the BRICK YARD, S.E. of MORLANCOURT on the BRAY - CORBIE Road.

At 12.30pm orders were issued to "B" Company, 50th M.G.Bn. to withdraw and rejoin their Battalion.

August 11th.

On completion of the operations the frontage held by the 58th Divn. was about 1800 yards. The M.G. defence was finally arranged as follows - 8 guns in the Forward Zone, 4 of which were in the front line. 1500 yards in rear of the front line 2 sections were disposed to form a main line of resistance and to put down a protective barrage.

From 300 - 500 yards in rear of this line 2 more sections were disposed as a close support to the main line of resistance and also within range to assist in the protective barrage.

The 8 guns in reserve at the BRICK YARD were given the role of replacing casualties or still further augmenting the defence in depth.

August 12th.

No operations were carried out. Positions further improved and consolidated.

August 13th.

In the early morning "B" Company was withdrawn to KEY WOOD, E. of PONT NOYELLES, "A" Company withdrawing in the evening to the same place. "D" and "C" Companies were relieved in the line on the night 13/14th by the 47th M.G.Bn., on relief proceeding to KEY WOOD.

COMMUNICATIONS.

Communications were maintained by use of Divisional lines to Brigades also runner relay posts with mounted orderlies from Companies to relay post and thence to Battalion by cycle orderly.

AMMUNITION SUPPLY.

Supply of ammunition was maintained by a succession of dumps from which companies drew, and maintained by pack and transport.

ENEMY MACHINE GUNS.

The use of captured enemy guns was found to work well as there was an unlimited supply of these as well as belt boxes for them.

REPAIR SHOP.

The establishing of an armourers repair shop at the runner relay post proved very useful, several guns being repaired and got into action in a very short space of time.

TRANSPORT.

On every occasion possible guns were moved forward almost to their positions by the use of pack and limber transport.

CASUALTIES.

OFFICERS..........3 Killed
2 Wounded
OTHER RANKS.......14 Killed
61 Wounded (5 have since rejoined).

ANIMALS...........1 Rider
26 Mules

LIMBERS G.S....... 2 destroyed by shell fire.

[signature] Lieut Col.

15.8.18 cmdg 58 Battalion M.G.Corps.

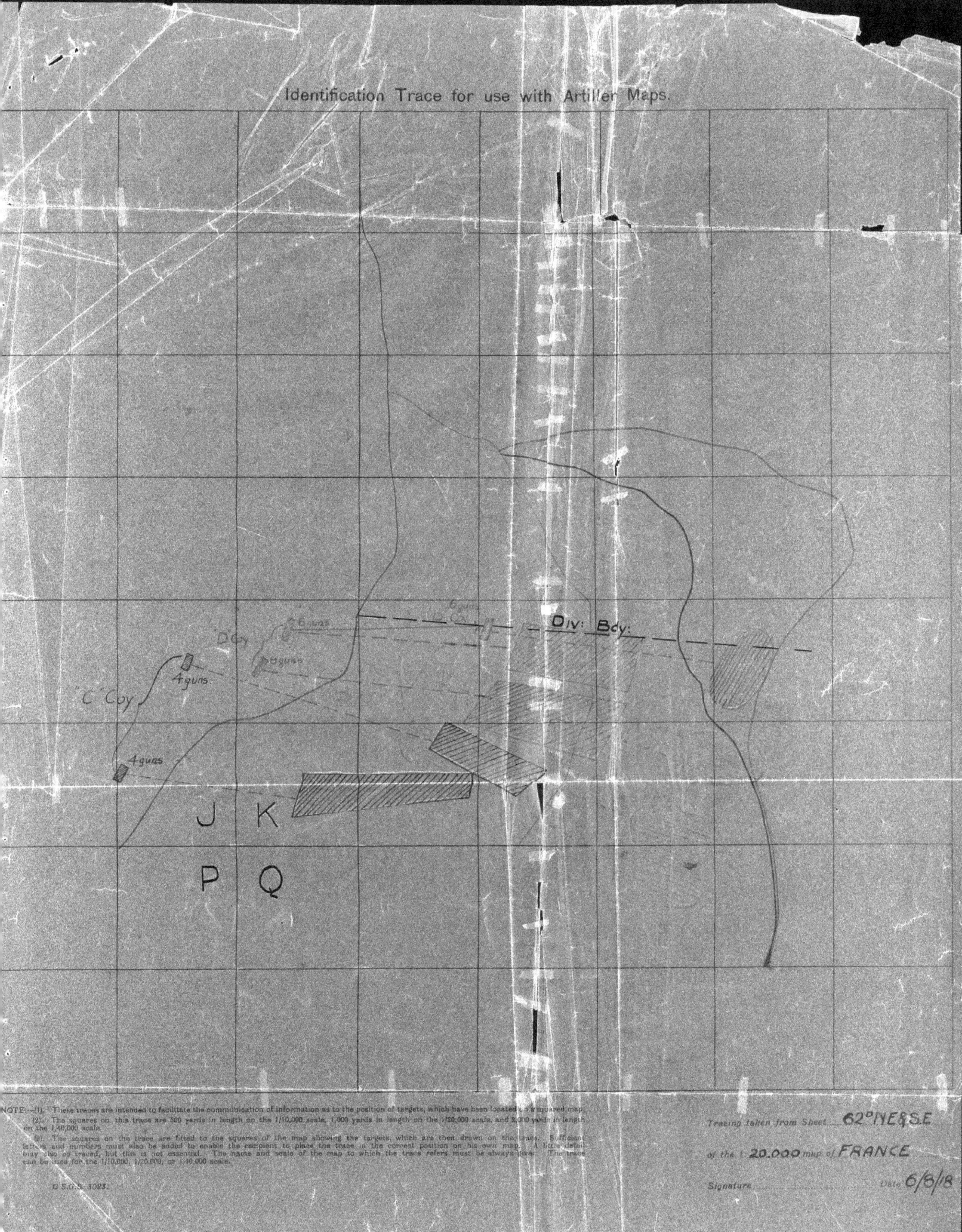
Identification Trace for use with Artiller Maps.
Div: Bdy:
6 guns
"D" Coy
"C" Coy
4 guns
4 guns
J K
P Q
NOTE:—(1). These traces are intended to facilitate the communication of information as to the position of targets, which have been located on a squared map.
(2). The squares on this trace are 500 yards in length on the 1/10,000 scale, 1,000 yards in length on the 1/20,000 scale, and 2,000 yards in length on the 1/40,000 scale.
(3). The squares on the trace are fitted to the squares of the map showing the targets, which are then drawn on the trace. Sufficient letters and numbers must also be added to enable the recipient to place the trace in the correct position on his own map. A little detail may also be traced, but this is not essential. The name and scale of the map to which the trace refers must be always given. The trace can be used for the 1/10,000, 1/20,000, or 1/40,000 scale.
G.S.G.S. 3023.
Tracing taken from Sheet 62D NE & S.E
of the 1 20.000 map of FRANCE
Signature
Date 6/8/18

COPY.

SECRET. FORTHCOMING OPERATIONS.

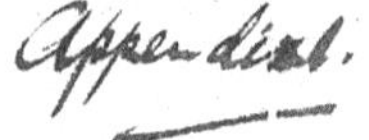

58th (LONDON) DIVISIONAL INSTRUCTIONS No.4.

MACHINE GUNS.

1. The Machine Guns will support the attack by covering fire and put down protective barrages during consolidation. They will as far as possible be employed in sections during the advance and where necessary after the final objective is reached, distributed in pairs in the Forward Zone.

2. For the attack on SAILLY LAURETTE, a section of "C" Company will be attached to the 2/10th London Regt. The task allotted to this Section will be to prevent any enemy movement along the Spur and the roads approaching the village through K.31 and K.32.

3. During the advance of 174th Inf Bde on the first objective, "D" Company of the M.G.Bn. and one Section of "C" Company will be allotted the task of searching by intense fire, the wood and ravines running in a S.W. direction from K.27 central.
The final barrage line for these guns will correspond to the outpost line of the first objective. Fire will cease on this line when our troops are due to reach the western edge of MALARD WOOD.

4. "B" Company of the M.G.Bn. attached to 174th Inf Bde will follow the advance of the Brigade as quickly as possible and take up positions to be able to carry out (a) the defence of the ground gained and (b) to cover the advance of 173rd Inf Bde to the final objective.
The O.C."B" Company M.G.Bn. will arrange the details under orders of 174th Inf Bde in consultation with 173rd Inf Bde.
8 guns of "D" Company on completion of their task will move forward to assist in accordance with para 6 below.

5. "A" Company of the M.G.Bn. will be under the orders of the B.G.C., 173rd Inf Bde for the purpose of consolidating the ground between the first and second objectives.
Arrangements should be made for harassing fire on the area E of the SOMME between MERICOURT-sur-SOMME and ETINEHEM.

6. 8 guns of "D" Company in addition to the task allotted in para 3 will be required to fill any gap which might take place on the Northern flank of the Division as the attack progresses. These 8 guns will consequently be in position on the left flank of the Division to to carry out their first task as in para 3 and when they move forward to assist "B" Company will take up a position for the purpose about K.28.a.0.7. The remaining 8 guns of "D" Company will remain in Position in Divisional Reserve.

7. 8 guns of "C" Company will be with 175th Inf Bde in Corps Reserve. The other 8 guns of this Company will rejoin them as soos as they can be released.

8. Full details as to duration of fire, timings, safetylimits, etc., will be issued to all concerned by the O.C. Machine Gun Battalion.

9. ACKNOWLEDGE.

(Sgd) C.M.DAVIS, Lieut-Colonel,
General Staff, 58th (London) Division.

5th August, 1918.

APPENDIX I.

SECRET. 58th BATTALION MACHINE GUN CORPS. COPY NO. 10.

ORDER NO. 23.

Ref. Map. Sheet. 62D 1/40,000. 1st August 1918.

1. 58th Battalion M.G.C. will be relieved by 12th Battalion M.G.C. as follows:-

"A" Coy. (ESBART FARM) on 2nd inst.
"C" Coy. (Left Brigade) on night 2/3rd inst.
"B" Coy.) (Right Brigade) on night 3/4th inst.
"D" Coy.)

2. Details for the relief will be arranged between Company Commanders concerned. All Defence Instructions, Maps etc. being handed over.

3. Receipts in duplicate will be forwarded to this office by noon 5th inst, care being taken that separate receipts for Reserve Rations are gi ven.

4. On relief, dismounted personnel will move by bus as follows. Companies in line will march direct to embussing point.

4. 2nd inst.
"A" Company.
With 174th Inf. Brigade Group embussing on BEHENCOURT-BAIZIEUX Road, head of column facing West, at Eastern outskirts of BEHENCOURT. Time 6.p.m. Destination. HALLOY LES PERNOIS taking over Billets occupied by "A" Coy. 12th Bn. M.G.C. Debussing on West Edge of HALLOY on HALLOY-BERTEAUCOURT Road.

3rd inst.
"C" Company.
With 173rd Inf. Brigade Group. Embussing point as above. Time 2.a.m. Destination BERTEAUCOURT taking over billets of "C" Company, 12th Bn. M.G.C. Debussing as above.

4th inst.
"B" & "D" Companies
With 175th Inf. Brigade Group. Embussing point as above. Time 2.a.m. Destination HAVERNAS. Debussing point VIGNACOURT-FLESSELES Road facing East.
Headquarters.
Move as above with 175th Brigade Group. Destination will be notified later.

5. Transport will march with Brigade Groups as follows. Time and route will be notified by respective Brigades.

2nd inst. "A" Coy. with 174th Brigade Group.
3rd inst. "C" Coy. " 173rd " "
4th inst. H.Q.)
"B" Coy.) " 175th " "
"D" Coy.)

6. Advance parties of 1 Officer and 3 O.Rs. will go in advance under Company arrangements, 1 day prior to Companies' move, arranging billets and guides etc ready for Companies' arrival.

7. All tentage will be handed over "in situ". Duplicate receipts being forwarded to this office.

8. Relief complete will be notified to Battalion H.Q. by Code Words "NO BEER".

9. Battalion H.Q. will close at ESBART FARM at 10.a.m 4th inst, and open at a place and time to be notified later.

10. ACKNOWLEDGE.

T. WATKINS. Capt & Adjt.

Distribution over.

Distribution.

1. 58th Division. "G".
2. 58th Division. "A" & "Q".
3. 173rd Inf. Bde.
4. 174th " "
5. 175th " "
6. O.C."A" Coy. 58th Bn.
7. O.C."B" Coy. " "
8. O.C."C" Coy. " "
9. O.C. "D" Coy. " "
10. C.O. 58th Bn.
11. S.O. " "
12. T.O. " "
13. Qr.Mr. " "
14. War Diary.
15. File.

SECRET. 58th BATTALION MACHINE GUN CORPS.

APPENDIX 2

ADDENDUM No. 1 to ORDER No. 24.

6th August 1918.

1. The following firework signals will be employed:-

(1) No. 32 Grenade, GREEN over GREEN over GREEN.... S.O.S.
(2) No. 32 Grenade, WHITE over WHITE over WHITE... SUCCESS SIGNAL i.e. OBJECTIVE GAINED.

2. O's. C. Companies and Sections will obtain ZERO hour from Brigades to which they are attached and will be responsible that watches are synchronised.

3. Battalion H.Q. will be with Advance Divisional H.Q. at J.19.c. where all reports will be sent.

C.J. WILEY. Lieut. Colonel.

Distribution.

All recipients of Order No. 24.

APPENDIX 2

SECRET. 58th BATTALION MACHINE GUN CORPS. Copy No. 16.

ORDER No. 24.

Ref. Map. 62 D. N.E. 1:20000
Local Map. 1:10000.

August 6th 1918.

1. Reference 58th Divisional Instructions No 4 dated 5th August. The attached map shows the tasks allotted to the Machine Guns detailed to support the advance by covering fire and the approximate positions of the Batteries.

2. For the attack on the First Objective fire will be opened at ZERO and maintained at the rate of 100 rounds a minute until the task is complete at ZERO plus 20 minutes.

3. The Section attached to 2/10th London Regiment will complete its task at ZERO plus 15 minutes.

4. During the consolidation of the First Objective the rate of fire will be 50 rounds a minute. This will be increased to 100 rounds a minute for 10 minutes when 173rd Infantry Brigade are passing through 174th Infantry Brigade for the advance on the Final objective.
Fire will cease at ZERO plus 145 minutes.

5. Officers Commanding Batteries in accordance with the above will prepare necessary charts and arrange for ammunition and water supply.

6. ACKNOWLEDGE.

C.J.WILEY. Lieut. Colonel.

Copy 1. to 58th Div G.
2. 173 Inf.Bde.
3. 174 Inf.Bde.
4. 175 Inf.Bde.
5. "A" Co. 58th Bn.M.G.C.
6. "B" do.
7. "C" do.
8. "D" do.
9. 18th M.G.Bn.
10. C.M.G.O.
11. 3rd Australian M.G.Bn.
12. 4th do.
13. O.C.58 M.G.Bn.
14. 2nd in Command 58 M.G.Bn
15. Signal Officer.58 Bn.
16. War Diary.
17. File.
18.19 Spare.

COPY

SECRET. FORTHCOMING OPERATIONS

58th (LONDON) DIVISIONAL INSTRUCTIONS No. 4.

MACHINE GUNS.

1. The Machine Guns will support the attack by covering fire and put down protective barrages during consolidation. They will as far as possible be employed in sections during the advance and where necessary after the final objective is reached, distrbuted in pairs in the Forward Zone.

2. For the attack on SAILLY LAURETTE, a section of "C" Company will be attached to the 2/10th London Regt. The task allotted to this Section will be to prevent any enemy movement along the Spur and the roads approaching the village through K 31 and K 32.

3. During the advance of 174th Inf.Brigade on the first objective, "D" Company of the M.G.Bn. and one Section of "C" Company will be allotted the task of searching by intense fire, the wood and ravines running in a S.W. direction from K 27 central.

The final barrage line for these guns will correspond to the outpost line of the first objective. Fire will cease on this line when our troops are due to reach the western edge of MALARD WOOD.

4. "B" Company of the M.G.Bn. attached to 174th Inf.Bde willl follow the advance of the Brigade as quickly as possible and take up positions to be able to carry out (a) the defence of the ground gained and (b) to cover the advance of 173rd Inf.Bde to the final objective.

The O.C. "B" Coy M.G.Bn will arrange the details under orders of 174th Inf.Bde in consultation with 173rd Inf.Brigade.

8 Guns of "D" Coy. on completion of their task will move forward to assist in accordance with para 6 below.

5. "A" Coy of the M.G.Bn will be under the orders of the B.G.C. 173rd Inf.Bde for the purpose of consolidating the ground between the First and second objectives.

Arrangemenas should be made for harassing fire on the area E of t the SOMME between MERICOURT-sur-SOMME and ETINEHEM.

6. 8 guns of "D" Company in addition to the task allotted in para.3 will be required to fill any gap which might take place on the Northern flank of the DIVISION as the attack progresses. These 8 guns will consequently be in position on the left flank of the Division to carry out their first task as in para.3 and when they move forward to assist "B" Coy. will take up a position for the purpose about K 27.a.0.7. The remaining 8 guns of "D" Coy will remain in position in Divisional Reserve.

7. 8 guns of "C" Coy will be with 175th Inf. Brigade in Corps Reserve. The other 8 guns of this Coy. will rejoin them as soon as they can be released.

8. Full details as to duration of fire, timings, safety limits, etc will be issued to all concerned by the O.C. Machine Gun Battalion.

9. ACKNOWLEDGE.

(Sgd) C.M.DAVIS. Lieut Colonel.
General Staff. 58th (London) Division.

5th August 1918.

SECRET

Operations of the 58th Division from 8 - 15 August 1918.

MACHINE GUNS.

1. On August 3rd the first intimation was received of the forthcoming attack on the Fourth Army front, and of the extent and nature of the task allotted to the 58th Division in those operations. On that date 2 Companies of the M.G.Battalion were still in the line but were to be relieved that night; the other 2 Companies were in the back areas.

2. On August 5th, after conferences between the Brigade Commanders and the M.G.Battalion Commander on the previous day, instructions were issued as to the employment of the Machine Guns in the attack. These instructions are contained in Appendix 1. On these a map and further instructions were issued to the M.G.Commanders concerned giving the tasks etc. allotted to the various companies. These included covering fire for the advance.

3. As secrecy was an essential factor to the success of the operations the preparation of the emplacements etc. could not be undertaken until the night of August 7/8. But it was possible to select the positions which were on a forward slope during daylight and to reach the assembly positions during the night of August 6/7.

4. The task of constructing emplacements, getting up ammunition, guns, water etc.starting at dusk on the evening of the 7th and having everything ready to open fire at 4.20am the following morning reflects great credit on the units concerned. Added to which there was a certain amount of liveliness due to the attacks and counter attacks on this front during the two days preceeding the attack; and a good many casualties to personnel and animals occurred.

August 8th.

Zero hour on the morning of the 8th the attack started in a thick mist which instead of clearing became thicker as the morning advanced. All guns taking part in the initial barrage carried out their tasks as arranged and "B" Company went forward behind the 174th Infantry Brigade to previously selected localities in order to consolidate and prepare for a secondary barrage in support of the 173rd Infantry Brigade, the latter being rendered most difficult owing to the heavy mist.

Two sections of "D" Company (allotted the dual task of taking part in the secondary barrage and if necessary to cover any gap that might take place between ourselves and the left flank Division) went forward and took up positions to carry out the secondary barrage, no gap having taken place.

"A" Company, allotted the task of supporting and consolidating the gains of the 173rd Infantry Brigade worked forward in close touch with the Infantry affording them good covering fire, and taking up good defensive positions.

Later in the day 2 sections of "C" Company from Corps Reserve moved forward to augment to M.G. defence in view of an expected counter-attack from the N.E. In addition to this the 2 sections of "D" Company in Divisional Reserve were also ordered forward to a more central position N.W. of MALARD WOOD.

The section of "C" Company allotted the task of covering and supporting the attack on SAILLY LAURETTE having carried out this task proceeded about 7pm to perform a similar operation as regards the attack on CHIPILLY. For this purpose the Section Commander considerably intensified his covering fire by utilising 3 German Machine Guns in addition to his own.

August 9th.
At 5.30pm the 175th Infantry Brigade and the 131st American Regt. attacked in a N.E. direction. For this purpose "C" Company had been assembled in the early afternoon, their role being to consolidate in depth the gains of the 175th Infantry Bde. This was carried out successfully, 2 sections taking up positions in the trenches of the old AMIENS defences.
On the afternoon of the 9th "B" Company, 50th M.G.Bn. was placed under orders of O.C. 58th M.G.Battalion. On arrival these guns were ordered to take up positions astride the boundary line between the 58th Division and the 131st American Regt. The positions were occupied before dawn on the 10th and arrangements completed for a protective barrage.

August 10th.
The 2 sections of "D" Company in Divisional Reserve were also sent forward to provide the defence in depth and put down a protective barrage in front of our new line. The remaining 2 sections of "D" Company becoming local reserve at the BRICK YARD, S.E. of MORLANCOURT on the BRAY - CORBIE Road.
At 12.30pm orders were issued to "B" Company, 50th M.G.Bn. to withdraw and rejoin their Battalion.

August 11th.
On completion of the operations the frontage held by the 58th Divn. was about 1800 yards. The M.G. defence was finally arranged as follows - 8 guns in the Forward Zone, 4 of which were in the front line. 1800 yards in rear of the front line 2 sections were disposed to form a main line of resistance and to put down a protective barrage.
From 300 - 500 yards in rear of this line 2 more sections were disposed as a close support to the main line of resistance and also within range to assist in the protective barrage.
The 8 guns in reserve at the BRICK YARD were given the role of replacing casualties or still further augmenting the defence in depth.

August 12th.
No operations were carried out. Positions further improved and consolidated.

August 13th.
In the early morning "B" Company was withdrawn to KEY WOOD, E. of PONT NOYELLES, "A" Company withdrawing in the evening to the same place. "D" and "C" Companies were relieved in the line on the night 13/14th by the 47th M.G.Bn., on relief proceeding to KEY WOOD.

COMMUNICATIONS.
Communications were maintained by use of Divisional lines to Brigades also runner relay posts with mounted orderlies from Companies to relay post and thence to Battalion by cycle orderly.

AMMUNITION SUPPLY.
Supply of ammunition was maintained by a succession of dumps from which companies drew, and maintained by pack and transport.

ENEMY MACHINE GUNS.
The use of captured enemy guns was found to work well as there was an unlimited supply of these as well as belt boxes for them.

REPAIR SHOP.
The establishing of an armourers repair shop at the runner relay post proved very useful, several guns being repaired and got into action in a very short space of time.

TRANSPORT.
On every occasion possible guns were moved forward almost to their positions by the use of pack and limber transport.

<u>CASUALTIES.</u>

OFFICERS.............3 Killed
2 Wounded
OTHER RANKS..........14 Killed
61 Wounded (5 have since rejoined).

ANIMALS..............1 Rider
28 Mules

LIMBERS G.S......... 2 destroyed by shell fire.

Lieut Col.

15.8.18 Cmdg 56 Battalion M.G.Corps.

Appendix 4

SECRET. **58th BATTALION, MACHINE GUN CORPS.** Copy No.....

ORDER No. 25.

August 21st, 1918.

1. "B" and "C" Companies will be prepared to move any time after 4.45.a.m. to-morrow the 22nd August, under instructions issued by the 174th and 175th Infantry Brigades to which they are attached respectively.

2. The 58th Battalion M.G.C. (less 2 Companies) will beready to move at 2 hours notice.

3. Water Tins will be filled to-night and the Water Carts will be filled up after providing for to-morrow morning's needs.

4. Surplus kit and Stores will be left in the wood beside "A" Coy's Guard Room.

5. Tent and bivouac covers will be collected at the same place.

6. ACKNOWLEDGE.

C.J.WILEY, Lieut-Colonel.

Distribution.over.

Distribution.

1. O.C. "A" Company.
2. O.C. "B" "
3. O.C. "C" "
4. O.C. "D" "
5. Signal Officer.
6. Transport Officer.
7. Quartermaster.
8. War Diary.
9. File.

NARRATIVE OF EVENTS

APPENDIX 4

for

AUGUST 21st - 31st 1918

MAP SHEET 62 D.

KEY WOOD 21st. Battalion was billeted in KEY WOOD. In the afternoon orders were received for B & C Coys to move with the 174 & 175 Inf. Bdes. respectively early on the following morning. The remainder of the Battn. was put on two hours notice to move.

22nd. 5.15am B Coy moved to the vicinity of HEILLY & joined the 174 Inf. Bde. group where they remained for the night.

5.30am C Coy moved with the 175 Inf. Brigade Group to J.14.b. & at 9.30 pm. in the evening the Coy moved into the line 2 sections in K.10 d & 16 b. and two sections in the OLD AMIENS defense line.

A & D Coy remained in KEY WOOD & carried out training.

23rd. At 4 am. A Coy left KEY WOOD & marched to MERICOURT-L'ABBÉ & joined the 173 Inf Bde. Group & later at 10.45 pm moved up & bivouaced in K 14 b & d just S. of MORLANCOURT. B Coy at 9 am. moved from HEILLY to DARWIN COPSE (D 17.c.). C Coy sections remained the same positions as on the previous day but at 10 30 pm. the Coy moved to their jumping off position for the attack on the next day L2 a & c. D Coy remained at KEY WOOD & carried out training.

HEILLY 24th. Battn H.Q. closed at Key Wood & relieved the 47 Batt. M.G.C. at HEILLY. One Coy of the 47th Batt. attached to the 140th Inf. Bde. remained in the line & came under orders of 58 Div.

HEILLY	24th	B Coy at 6 am moved with the 174 Inf Bde Group into the trenches S.W. of Morlancourt (K13) and at night two sections moved to the assembly point at K5.x11. At 1 am the 175 Inf Bde with C Coy attacked & gained all objectives. At 6am D Coy moved from KEY WOOD to J9 central being in Divisional Reserve. A Coy moved at night with the 173 Inf Bde to assembly position NE of GRESSAIRE WOOD. B Coy & C Coy of 2nd Life Gds M.G Batt. attached to 140 & 175 Inf Bdes respectively. Operation orders issued for a renewed attack on the following morning	Map SHEET 62D
K14 central	25th	Battalion H.Q. moved from HEILLY to K14 central.	
	1am	Green Line captured by 140 & 175 Inf Bdes. 1 Coy 2nd Life Gds M.G. Batt. moved up & took over positions of C Coy who withdrew to the immediate rear.	
	10am	173 Inf Bde attacked & passed through & on reaching their final objective they were not in touch with the enemy. An Advance Guard was formed & continued on but was checked by hostile artillery & M.G fire along the BRAY-MARICOURT Road resistance being particularly strong at BONFRAY FARM & BILLON WOOD. At 9am B Coy moved with 174 Inf Bde Group to valley in L3 & thence to F29 in readiness for the advance on the following morning.	

K central 25th (Contd).

D Coy moved up to the BRICKYARD K15d 5.1. | MAP SHEET 62D
The 140 Inf. Bde. & B & C Coys 2nd Life Gds M.G. Batt came under the orders of the 47th Division

26th A Coy. with the 173rd Inf. Bde moved forward & occupied positions in front of BILLON WOOD & BOISERAY FARM where they remained throughout the day.

B Coy took up positions W. of BILLON WOOD in F30 a & c.

C Coy assembled & reformed at L4a.

D Coy moved from the BRICKYARD to F20a & three sections were placed under the 173 Inf Bde. & one section under 174 Inf Bde but later the Coy. again reverted to Divisional Reserve.

27th 173 & 174 Inf. with A & B Coys advanced forming a line S. of MARICOURT & also taking the village. MAP SHEET 62C

C Coy moved forward to F30a & D Coy was placed under orders of the 175 Inf Bde. for a few hours but in the afternoon again came under orders of O.C. 58th M.G. Battn. At about 5pm they were then ordered to take up two positions of 8 guns each at A22a & A16a. Harassing fire was then carried from 10pm. to 5.15 am. MAP SHEET 62D & SHEET 62C

L1b 28th Battalion H.Q. closed at K14 central & opened at L1b. MAP SHEET 62D

A Coy with 173 Inf. Bde. again attacked & occupied a line in front of BOIS d'en HAUT MAP SHEET 62C

A 19 Central.

31st. 1000 yards W. of BOUCHAVESNES. Orders given for C Coy to withdraw to A 22 a 7c.

MAP SHEET 62D

SHEET 62C

L1b. 28th. B Coy with 174 Inf Bde also attacked in the evening C Coy with 175 Inf Bde had orders to take over the line from the 173 + 174 Inf. Bdes. For this purpose D Coy was attached to 175 Inf Bde MAP SHEET 62 C.

On the night 28/29th 175 Inf. Bde with C + D Coys moved up + took up positions + on completion A Coy withdrew to F23a + B Coy to valley A27a. B + C Coys of 2nd Life Gds M.G. Battn again came under orders of 58th Division + were ordered to take up defensive positions E. of BILLON WOOD. MAP SHEET 62 D. + SHEET 62 C.

29th A Coy in valley F28d B Coy in valley A27a. C Coy + D Coy in line with 175 Inf Bde. Enemy reported to be retreating rapidly. MAP SHEET 62 D. + SHEET 62 C.

A19. Central 30th Battalion HQ. closed at L1b. + opened at A19b Advance continued 175 Inf Bde + C+D Coys. in the Advance Guard B Coy moved with the 174 Inf Bde group by bus to HEM WOOD on evening of 30th + assembly positions taken up. A Coy remained in valley F28d C+D Coys carried out harassing fire by night. B + C Coys 2nd Life Gds M.G. Batt came under orders of the O.C. 2nd Life Gds M.G. Batt.

31st. 174 Inf Bde with B Coy attacked a line E of MARRIERES WOOD objectives gained D Coy in line with 74 Bde. A Coy moved up in the evening to HEM WOOD. + from there moved to assembly positions

21 SECRET

To 58 Div. "A"

Herewith original War Diary of the Battalion under my command from 1.8.1918 - 31.8.1918.

September 9th 1918.

Cpreey Lieut Col.
Commanding 58th Bn M.G.C.

14

Instructions regarding War Diaries and Intelligence Summaries are contained in F. S. Regs., Part II. and the Staff Manual respectively. Title Pages will be prepared in manuscript.

WAR DIARY

or

~~INTELLIGENCE SUMMARY~~

(Erase heading not required.)

Army Form C. 2118.

58th Battalion
Machine Gun Corps
September 1st – 30th
1918

YR 7

Place	Date	Hour	Summary of Events and Information	Remarks and references to Appendices
A19b n. CARNOY	1st		On the early morning the 173 Inf Bde with A Coy attacked gaining their objectives GERMAIN TRENCH and ANGORA TRENCH, covering fire for the attack being given by D Coy.	Sheet 62c N.W.
			At night A Coy being relieved by a coy of 74th M.G. Battn marched to the valley in B13d. remaining there till the following day. B Coy withdrew with the 174th Inf Bage to HINDLEG WOOD and D Coy proceeded to HILL 110. C Coy remained at rest in the valley in A22 a + c.	
B19 central	2nd	9 am	Battalion Headquarters closed at A19b and opened at B19 central. All Coys again came under orders of OC 58th M.G. Battn and moved to the vicinity of BATTERY COPSE	
	3rd 4th + 5th		Coys remained in same place, rested and refitted and carried out training under orders of OC Companies.	
	6th – 25		inclusive See Appendix 1.	

2449 Wt. W14957/M90 750,000 1/16 J.B.C. & A. Forms/C.2118/12.

Army Form C. 2118.

Instructions regarding War Diaries and Intelligence Summaries are contained in F. S. Regs., Part II. and the Staff Manual respectively. Title pages will be prepared in manuscript.

WAR DIARY
or
~~INTELLIGENCE SUMMARY.~~
(Erase heading not required.)

58th Battalion
Machine Gun Corps
Sept 1st – 30th

Place	Date	Hour	Summary of Events and Information	Remarks and references to Appendices
CATERPILLER WOOD.	26th		The whole Battn less 'B' Coy marched to MERICOURT L'ABBEE and there B Coy joined the HQ. A + B Coys proceeded by No 5 train and C + D Coy by train No 6 to 'ACQ'. Transport also proceeded by train	Sheets 57c 62D & 44B
GRAND SERVINS.	27th		Battalion arrived at 'ACQ' and proceeded by route march to GOUY SERVINS All companies being billeted in the neighbourhood. GOUY GRAND & PETIT SERVINS. Coy Commanders proceeded up the line to reconnoitre, orders being received to take over the line on the following day this was however postponed for 24 hours	Sheet 44B.
	28th		Reconnaissance carried out by Coy and Section Commanders. Battalion remained in billets at SERVINS.	
FOSSE 2	29th		Battalion HQ closed at GRAND SERVINS and opened at FOSSE 2 relieving the 24th MG Battalion. All Coys embussed at GOUY SERVINS and proceeded to LES BREBIS. The line being taken over in the evening from 24th MG Bn. AB.C Coys with 12 guns each in the line and 4 in Reserve and D Coy in Divisional Reserve at FOSSE 2.	APPENDIX I Sheets 44B & 44A
	30th		ABC Coys in the line D Coy in Div Reserve.	

D Rankin. Major for Lt Col
Commanding 58 Bn M.G. Corps

D. D. & L., London, E.C. (A7841) Wt. W5o/M1672 350,000 4/17 Sch. 52a Forms/C2118/14

APPENDIX I.

Narrative of Events from September 6–25th

58th Battalion Machine Gun Corps

DATE		Ref Maps
B19 central (1st BATTERY COPSE) Sept. 6th	On orders being received that the Division would relieve the 47th Division, all companies were placed with their respective Brigades D. Coy being placed in Divisional reserve. B Coy joined the 174 Bde group and embussed at HEM WOOD and proceeded to MOISLAINS proceeding from there they marched to the vicinity of D.15 where they remained until the evening of the 7th. C. Coy embussed in the afternoon and proceeded with the 175 Bde into the line taking over the whole Divisional front from the 140 and 141 Bdes of the 47th Div. D. Coy remained at B19 in reserve. During the day orders were received that A Coy would be prepared to move with the 173 Bde group on the following day. Two Coys 100th MG Battn were taken over and came under orders of 58th Battn MGC one being in reserve at BOUCHAVESNES and the other attached to 'C' Coy	62c NW. 57c SE. 44a NW3 44a SW1.
Sept. 7th	Battalion HQ closed at B19 central, and opened near QUARRY (BOUCHAVESNES.) In conjunction with the attack of the 74th Div on the right in view of establishing themselves on the BLUE LINE, the 175 Bde also attacked supported by 'C' Coy 58th and 'D' Coy 100th MG Battn. At 7am 'A' Coy embussed with the 173 Bde group near HEM WOOD for the purposes of moving D Coy were attached to 173 Bde and embussed with them but on the completion of the move they again reverted to command of O.C. 58th MGBn. A Coy on debussing moved to D13 and remained there for the day but in the evening moved up to position near NURLU. D Coy moved to QUARRY (D15a 2.7) and B Coy 100th MG Battn were attached to them and moved from BOUCHAVESNES to QUARRY. In the evening 2 section of D Coy along with 2 sects B Coy 100th proceeded into the line in W25a. to carry out harassing fire with 174 Bde	

Narrative of Events from September 6th – 25th   58th Batt Machine Gun Corps

Sept 8th

Battalion H.Q. closed at BOUCHAVESNES and opened at EPINETTE WOOD (D15d 65.55).

At dawn the 174 Bde with B. Coy moved forward through the 175 Bde and 12th Div covering the whole Divisional front. The 2 sect. B Coy 100th and 2 sect D Coy assisted by covering fire.

A. Coy with the 173 Bde moved in close support of 174 Bde with one Coy 100th attached to the 173 Bde.

C Coy, after the 174 Bde passed through, withdrew with the 175 Bde to a bivouac area, being in Divisional Reserve.

The remaining two Coys of the 100th M.G. Batt came under orders of the O.C. 58th Batt. M.G.C.

The result of the 174 Bde attack, they reached the outskirts of EPHY & PEZIERES

Sept 9th

During the day no operations were undertaken on account of the weather.

In the evening the two sect. of B Coy 100th in the line were relieved by the two section of D Coy from rear, on relief the whole of B Coy 100th was situated in the QUARRY (D15b).

Sept 10th

The 173 Bde with ½ A. Coy attacked in the early morning with a view to capturing EPHY & PEIZIERES heavy fighting took place but although our infantry gained a footing in both of the above mentioned villages they were driven back, succeeding however in still retaining TOTTENHAM POST.

Attached to the 173 Bde for the attack 12 Guns of C Coy 100th and 2 sect A Coy 58th. whilst the remaining 2 sects of A Coy were used for Barrage work and after the task allotted them came under orders of the 173 Bde. D Coy and 2 sects. A Coy 100th. also were employed for Barrage work.

See Appendix A.

Narrative of Events from September 6th – 25th

58th Batt. Machine Gun Corps

Sept. 10th In the evening A Coy 100th M.G. Battn withdrew to vicinity of GUYENCOURT and came under orders of 175 Bde. At night B. Coy withdrew to the vicinity of LIERAMONT where they remained till the 15th.

Sept 11 D. Coy placed at the disposal of B.G.C. 173 Bde. who were in the line supported by A Coy and C Coy 100th.

At night the 175 Bde took over the whole of the Divisional front from 173 Bde. C Coy relieved A Coy and A Coy 100th came into reserve under orders of B.G.C. 175. D Coy also remained in the line and came under orders of B.G.C 175. O.C. C Coy took over command of all M.G. on the Divn front in the line. Appendix. B.

A Coy on relief proceeded to LIERAMONT vicinity. Orders being issued that they were under command of B.G.C 173 and must be prepared to take up defensive positions when ordered.

Sept 12–14 Vottenham POST retaken by a raid of the enemy. 175 Bde. remained in the line.

Sept 15. On the night of 15th–16th the 174 Bde and B Coy moved up and relieved 175 Bde & C Coy. Appendix C
B Coy relieved 2 sections D. Coy and 2 section 100th Coy at JACAUVENNE COPSE.
A Coy/100 relieved C Coy 58th
2 sections D Coy relieved 1 section B Coy 100th
B Coy 100 moved to E 2 a & c
C Coy on relief moved to EPINETTE WOOD

Sept 16 Orders issued for the attack to be continued at a date & hour to be notified later. Appendix D
Orders issued to the M.G. as to the part they would play. B & D Coys being retained under orders of O.C 58th for Barrage fire.

Narrative of Events from September 6th – 25th

58th Bn. Machine Gun Corps

Date	Narrative	Remarks
Sept. 17	Further orders issued regarding the forthcoming attack which would start on the following day over a very large front. At dusk. A Coy moved forward to their assembly positions in readiness. Command of 100th M. G. Batn passed to 12th Division	
Sept. 18.	The attack started at 5.20 a.m. on a very large front. A Coy with the 173 Bde and two section of D. Coy also moving forward to consolidate. B Coy and the remaining two section of D Coy fired the covering Barrage. C Coy moved forward in Corps reserve to vicinity of GUYENCOURT. Much opposition met with and objectives not reached. B Coy moved to LIERAMONT	
Sept. 19.	In the event of the infantry pushing forward patrols and being able to advance arrangements were made to put down a barrage with the object of gaining KILDARE POST	Appendix E
Sept 20	As a result of the attack on the previous day POPLAR Tr was reported taken after great enemy resistance. At night the 175 Bde relieved the 173 Bde but only one section C Coy proceeded with them to attack on the following day. All A Coy remained in the line till the following day.	Appendix F & G
Sept. 21st	The 175 Bde in conjunction with the 12th & 33 Div. attacked with a view to pushing on as far as possible. B Coy was put on ½ hours notice to move any time after 7 a.m. Later in the day the remaining three sections of 'C' Coy moved forward and relieved A. Coy. who withdrew to vicinity of LIERAMONT.	

Narrative of Events from Sept 6th – 25th

58th Battalion Machine Gun Corps
Appendix

Sept 21. D Coy and 3 sect A Coy supported the attack with covering fire with Barrages as shown in appendix.

Sept 22nd. Attack still continued in conjunction with the 33rd. The objective of previous day now gained. KILDARE Post & KILDARE LANE. and also along DADOS LANE & HOLTS TRENCH. In the evening the two section of B Coy moved up into the line taking up positions at ORCHARD POST & TOINE POST.

In the evening of 22/23. D Coy withdrew to reserve.

Sept 23rd. The remaining two section of B Coy now moved into the line taking up position in F 28 a. The Div with the exception of 174 Bde & B now was out of the line and arrangements were made for the Div to embuss to a rear area. Orders being issued in the afternoon.

Sept 24. At 5am the Battalion less B. Coy embussed on the VILLERS FAUCON road and proceeded to CATERPILLAR WOOD where they stayed rested for two days till the 26th

In the evening B Coy with 174 Bde group were withdrawn to VILLERS FAUCON and remained there till the following morning

Sept 25th. B Coy embussed and proceeded to billets at HEILLY the transport proceeding by road. On arrival the Coy came again under orders of OC 58th Batt MGC.

Remainder of Battn remained at CATERPILLAR WOOD.

APPENDIX H.

APPENDIX A

SECRET. 58th BATTALION MACHINE GUN CORPS

MACHINE GUN INSTRUCTIONS.

1. 173 BRIGADE will have attached to it 12 Machine Guns of "C" Company, 100 M.G. Battalion; and 2 Sections of "A" Company, 58 M.G. Battalion. The 2 Sections of "A" Company on completion of the task allotted to them by the O.C., M.G. Battalion will come under the orders of 173 BRIGADE.

2. "D" Company 58th Battalion and 2 Sections of "C" Company, 100th Bn, and 2 Sections of "A" Company 58th Bn, will under instructions of the O.C., 58th M.G. Bn be employed for covering fire to the advance and for a protective barrage during consolidation.

3. 8 guns of the 100th Bn and 4 Guns of "D" Company 58th Bn will be in position about W 29 c.4.5. to cover the advance of the left Bn. Barrage line will start from W 30 b.5.7. to X 25 c.0.4.

12 guns of "D" Company 58th Bn. will be in position about E 11 central. to cover the advance of the Right Bn. Barrage line will start from F 1 a.6.5. to F 1 d.3.3.

The protective barrage line will be from X 25 b 2.8. to F 2 a. 7.5.

4. 8 guns of "A" Company 58th Bn. will be in position about E 4 d.9.5. to barrage the gap in the Artillery barrage. Start line road from E 6 d.8.9. to W 30 d.4.0. finishing on the Railway between F 1 a.8.9. and X 25 c.7.3. Fire will remain on start line for 15 minutes and move forward 100 yards in five minutes.

5. Time Tables will be issued direct to the M.G. Group Commanders.

6. It is hoped to arrange for 4 guns of "B" Company 58th M.G. Bn. to barrage the trenches in F 1 b.

7. Zero hour 5.15 a.m. September 10th 1918.

September 9th 1918.

C.J. WILEY. Lieut Col.
Commanding 58th Bn. M.G.C.

Copies issued to:-

No 1. "A" Co. 58 M.G. Bn.
2 "B" Co do.
3. "D" Co do.
4. "C" Co 100 M.G. Bn.
5. 173rd Inf. Bde.
6 174th " "
7. War Diary.
8. File.

Appendix B

SECRET. 58th BATTALION MACHINE GUN CORPS.

Whilst the 175 Infantry Brigade are holding the line the O.C. "C" Co 58th M.G.Bn will be in command of all the M.G's on the Divisional front.

The B.G.C. 175 Infantry Brigade will issue orders to "D" Co 58th Bn and "C" Co 100th Bn through O.C. "C" Co. 58th Bn.

A dump of M.G. Ammunition is being formed at the H.Q. of "D" Co 58th Bn E 3 a.8.0. This dump must be replenished as it is drawn from.

O.C. "C" Company is arranging for continuous harrassing fire under instructions already issued to him and it is of vital importance that this is carried on night and day. Certificates will be sent at 9.a.m. daily to O.C. "C" Co showing the number of rounds fired (a) between 6 a.m. and 6.p.m. and (b) 6.p.m. and 6.a.m. of the previous 24 hours.

September 12th 1918.

Lieut Col.
Commanding 58th Bn.M.G.C.

Copies issued to:-
O.C. "C" Co 58 Bn.
O.C. "D" Co 58 Bn.
O.C. "C" Co 100 Bn.
O.C. 100th M.G.Bn.

SECRET. 58th BATTALION MACHINE GUN CORPS. Copy No. 2.

OPERATION ORDER NO.32. APPENDIX C.

Ref. 57 C. S.E. 1/20000 Sept.15th 1918.
Sheet. 62 C. N.E. "

1. The following reliefs of Machine Gun Companies will take place.

2. "B" Co.58th Bn will relieve two Sections of "D" Co. 58th Bn in the front line and two Sections of "B" Co. 100th Bn. at JACAUVENNE COPSE tonight 15/16th September.

3. "A" Co.100th Bn. will relieve "C" Company 58th Bn. on the night 16/17th September.

4. On relief 2 Sections of "D" Co. will move to W 28 central relieving one Section of "B" Co. 100th Bn.
"B" Co. 100th Bn on relief will move to E 2 a and c.
"C" Co. 58th Bn. on relief will move to EPINETTE WOOD.

5. O.C. "B" Co 58th Bn. will be in command of all the Machine Guns on the Divisional Front under orders of B.G.C. 174th INFANTRY BRIGADE on completion of the relief tonight.

6. Completion of reliefs to be reported to 174 and 175 INFANTRY BRIGADES and to O.C. 58th M.G.Bn.

Distribution over.

C.J.WILEY. Lieut Col.
Commanding 58th Bn.M.G.C.

Copy No 1. 58th Div."G"
2. 174 Inf.Bde.
3. 175 Inf.Bde.
4. O.C."B" Co.58 Bn.
5. O.C."C" do.
6. O.C."D" do.
7. O.C."A" Co 100th Bn.
8. O.C."B" Co 100th Bn.
9. O.C.58th Bn.
10. O.C.100th Bn.
11. War Diary.
12. File.

APPENDIX D

58th BATTALION MACHINE GUN CORPS.

MACHINE GUNS.

1. The attack will be supported by a Machine Gun Barrage and for which "B" and "D" Companies will be under the orders of the O.C. 58th M.G.Battalion.

2. Two Batteries of 8 machine guns each will be in position in W 29 a and c. to put down a creeping barrage 500 yards in front of the Artillery Barrage as far East as the grid line between Squares X 25 and X 26.

3. Two Batteries of 4 guns each in W 29 d and E 5 b. will commence fire at Zero plus 5 minutes on the line of the Railway and search Eastwards finishing on POPLAR TRENCH as the Artillery Barrage reaches the grid line between Squares X 25 and 26.

4. Two Sections of "D" Company at E 4 d. 7.5. will move at Zero by the road running N.E. by McPHEE Post and take up positions at about X 25 a.3.9 and X 25 a.5.5. and will search the valleys NORTH and EAST of the objective until new Zero.

5. The other 2 Sections of "D" Company on finishing the creeping barrage will move to positions about X 25 c.5.8. and X 25 c.9.2.

6. "D" Company on arriving in the above positions will come under the orders of 173 INFANTRY BRIGADE.

7. One Section of "B" Company on finishing its barrage will move to the Sunken Road at W 30 a.8.3. and search the valleys round X 20 central until new Zero.

September 16th 1918.

[signature] Lt Colonel

SECRET. 58th BATTALION MACHINE GUN CORPS. Copy No. 14

OPERATION ORDER NO.33.

Ref.
SHEETS. 57 C.S.E.
62 C.N.E.

1. "B" and "D" Companies of the 58th M.G.Bn. will be under the orders of the O.C. 58th M.G.Bn. for covering fire in the attack on Z day. "C" Company will be in Divisional Reserve.

2. The attached sketch shows the position of Batteries on Y - Z night and the tasks allotted to them. The guns in the JACQVENNE COPSE are should if possible select positions as follows, the 8 guns of "B" Coy at W 29 a.5.5. and the 8 guns of "D" Coy at W 29 c.6.5.

3. The 2 Sections of "D" Coy at E 4 d.7.5. will be ready with limbers to move at ZERO along the road leading to McPHEE POST thence to railway at W 30 a.9.7. 1 Section will take up position about X 19 c.1.1. to cover the ground towards 19 central. 1 Section will take up position at X 25 a.3.6. to cover the ground eastwards and the valley north eastwards. Up till 3 hours 40 minutes from ZERO they will also search PIGEON RAVINE and the whole of Square X 21 d, after which they will come under 173 BRIGADE.

4. One Section of "B" Coy at W 29 a.5.5. will be ready to move with limbers at ZERO plus 50 minutes i.e. after completion of its barrage, to the road triangle at W 30 a.7.2. and when in position will search the ground N.E. of a line between X 20 a.8.0. and X 20 d.0.6. to a depth of 500 yards. Fire will cease at ZERO plus 3 hours 20 minutes at the far edge of this area creeping forward from the near edge at ZERO plus 3 hours 10 minutes.

The Section of "B" Company remaining at W 29 a. will concentrate on a line from X 26 a.0.4. to X 26 a.0.9. from ZERO plus 45 to ZERO plus 70 minutes.

5. The 2 Sections of "D" Company at W 29 c. will on completion of barrage at ZERO plus 45 minutes move forward to X 25 c. One Section in position about X 25 c.7.7. and one Section about X 25 c.9.2. They will then come under the orders of 173 BRIGADE.

6. "B" Coy will remain in its positions until further orders.

7. Rate of fire: Guns firing on Red Barrage lines, one belt in 3 mins, throughout. Guns firing on Green lines one belt in 4 minutes on 1st and 2nd lines and 1 in 3 minutes on 3rd and 4th lines. Ammunition supply will be arranged accordingly.

8. "B" Company will establish a dump of 20,000 rounds S.A.A. at the road junction W 30 a.2.2. by ZERO plus 3 hours.

9. Z day and ZERO hour will be notified later to all concerned by an Officer orderly who will also give the correct time.

C.J.WILEY Lieut Col.
Commanding 58th Bn.M.G.C.

Issued at.

"B" Co.	1 and 2)		174 Inf.Bde.	9.	
"D" Co.	3 and 4)	with map	175 Inf.Bde.	10.	
173 Inf.Bde.	5)		12 Div.M.G.Bn.	11.	with map.
58th Div. G.	6.		21 " "	12.	with map.
"A" Co.	7.	with map.	O.C.58 M.G.Bn.	13.	
"C" Co.	8.		Diary.	14.	

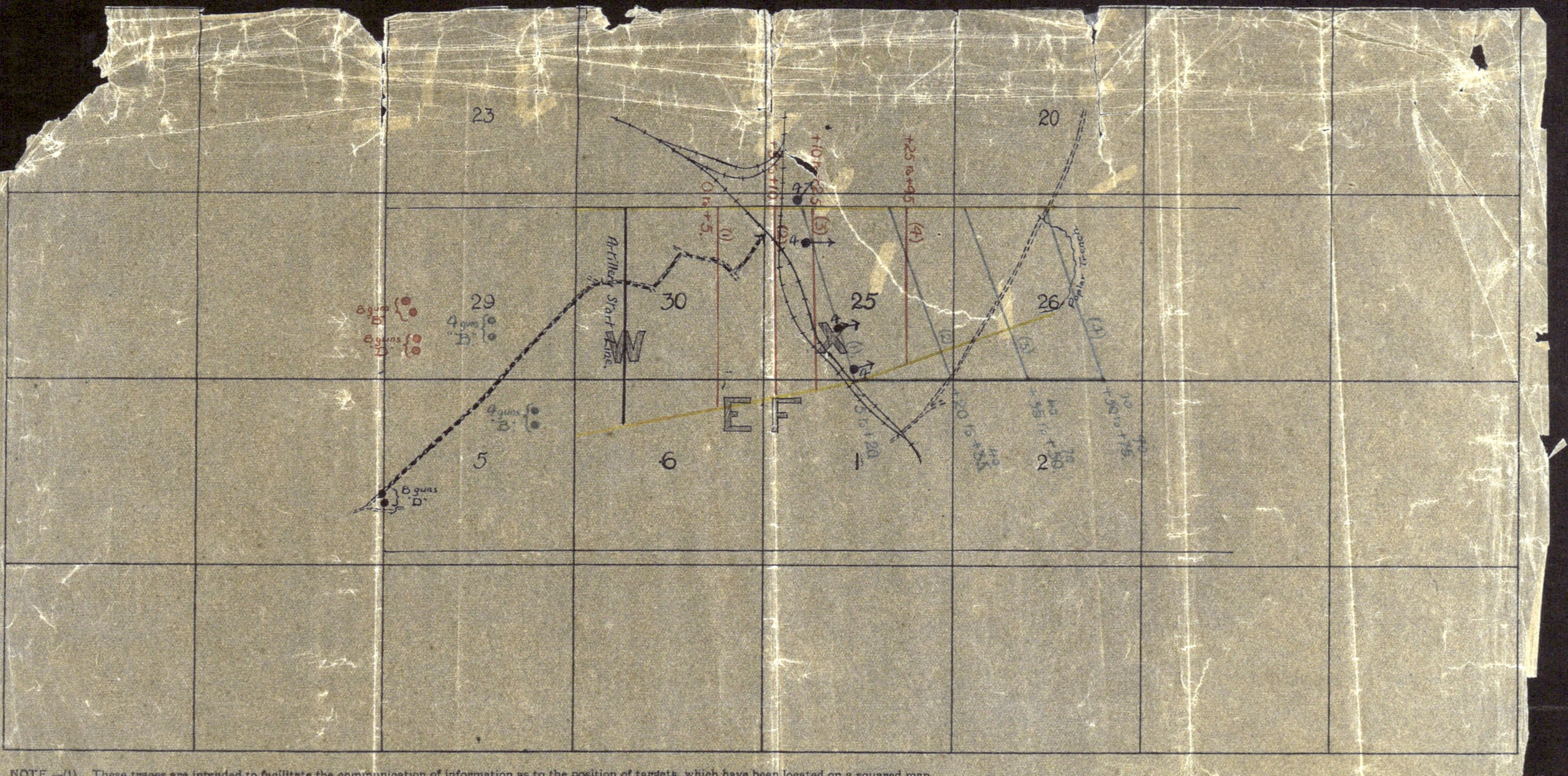

NOTE.—(1). These traces are intended to facilitate the communication of information as to the position of targets, which have been located on a squared map.

(2). The squares on this trace are 500 yards in length on the 1/10,000 scale, 1,000 yards in length on the 1/20,000 scale, and 2,000 yards in length on the 1/40,000 scale.

(3). The squares on the trace are fitted to the squares of the map showing the targets, which are then drawn on the trace. Sufficient letters and numbers must also be added to enable the recipient to place the trace in the correct position on his own map. A little detail may also be traced, but this is not essential. The name and scale of the map to which the trace refers must be always given. The trace can be used for the 1/10,000, 1/20,000, or 1/40,000 scale.

G.S.G.S. 3023.

Tracing taken from Sheets 57c S.E. & 62c N.E.

of the 1:20,000 map of FRANCE.

Signature .... Date 16/9/18.

APPENDIX "E"

SECRET.

58th BATTALION MACHINE GUN CORPS. Copy No..

OPERATION ORDER No.34.

Ref. 57 C.S.E. 1:20000
Sheets 62 C.N.E. 1:20000

September 19.1918.

1. Should a Battalion of the 58th Division advance to KILDARE POST this evening or tomorrow the Machine Guns of "D" Company and One Section of "A" Company will fire a covering barrage.

2. The Two Sections of "D" Company in X 25 c. will search 200 yards N and S. of the Grid Line starting at X 27 central and ending at X 28 central.

3. The Two Sections of "D" Company in X 25 a will move forward to about junction of FIR SUPPORT and BEECH AVENUE and will search from a line joining X 27 d.0.3. and X 21 d.0.2. eastwards to the road running through X 28 b. central.

4. One Section of "A" Company from a position as far East as possible in X 26 a. will search the Sunken Road known as CATELET TRENCH.

Issued to
"D" Co.58 M.G.Bn.
"A" do.
173 Inf.Bde.

C.J. WILEY. Lieut Col.
Commanding 58th Bn.M.G.C.

APPENDIX F.

War Diary

SECRET. **58th BATTALION MACHINE GUN CORPS.** Copy No...

OPERATION ORDER No.35.

Ref. 57 C. S.E. 1:20000.
Sheets. 62 C. N.E. 1:20000.

September 20th 1918.

1. 175 BRIGADE will attack tomorrow morning along the Northern slopes of LARK SPUR and occupy KILDARE POST.

2. "D" Company and 3 Sections of "A" Company 58th Bn.M.G.C. will cover the advance by Machine Gun fire.

3. The 3 Sections of "A" Company will be in POPLAR TRENCH. Their task is marked in Blue on the sketch.
   Two Sections of "D" Company will move to BEECH AVENUE, X 25 b. Their task is in Red.
   The two Sections of "D" Company in X 25 c. will perform the task in Green.

4. The necessary positions and charts for the above will be prepared at once.

5. The exact start line and times will be issued later.

6. Rate of fire will be 250 rounds in 3 minutes.

7. Machine Guns of 12th Division on the right and 33rd Division on the left ~~xxxx~~ are co-operating.

C.J.WILEY. Lieut Col.
Commanding 58th Bn.M.G.C.

Distribution over.

War Diary

Issued to

x 1. O.C. "A" Co 58th Bn.
x 2. O.C. "D" Co 58th Bn.
x 3. 175 Inf.Bde.
4. 173 Inf.Bde.
x 5. 58th Div. "G"
x 6. O.C.58th Bn.
7. War Diary.
8. File.
x 9. 33 Bn.M.G.C.
x 10. 12 Bn.M.G.C.

Maps issued to x

NOTE.—(1). These traces are intended to facilitate the communication of information as to the position of targets, which have been located on a squared map.

(2). The squares on this trace are 500 yards in length on the 1/10,000 scale, 1,000 yards in length on the 1/20,000 scale, and 2,000 yards in length on the 1/40,000 scale.

(3). The squares on the trace are fitted to the squares of the map showing the targets, which are then drawn on the trace. Sufficient letters and numbers must also be added to enable the recipient to place the trace in the correct position on his own map. A little detail may also be traced, but this is not essential. The name and scale of the map to which the trace refers must be always given. The trace can be used for the 1/10,000, 1/20,000, or 1/40,000 scale.

G.S.G.S. 3023.

Tracing taken from Sheet 57c S.E.

of the 1: 20,000 map of FRANCE.

Signature .... Date 20/9/18.

APPENDIX G

SECRET.

58th BATTALION MACHINE GUN CORPS. Copy No.5.

OPERATION ORDER No.36.

Ref. 57 C. S.E. 1:20000
Sheets. 62 C. N.E. 1:20000

20th September 1918.

1. The Artillery Start Line is 100 yards East of the Grid Line dividing Squares X 26 and 27 and moves at the rate of 100 yards in 4 minutes dwelling for 10 minutes on the Start Line and 16 minutes on the objective.

2. ZERO is at 5.40.a.m.

3. All Batteries will open fire at ZERO. The Green Battery will cease fire at ZERO plus 30 minutes on its extreme range The Red Battery will cease fire at ZERO plus 60 minutes on its Eastern edge.

The Blue Battery will cease fire on its Eastern edge at ZERO plus 95 minutes.

C.J. RILEY. Lieut Col.
Commanding 58th Bn.M.G.Corps.

Issued to
1. O.C."A" Co.58 Bn.
2. O.C."D" Co.58 Bn.
3. 175 Inf.Bde.
4. O.C.58 Bn.
5. War Diary.
6. File.

APPENDIX H.

SECRET. 58th BATTALION, MACHINE GUN CORPS. Copy No...9...

ORDER No. 37.

Ref. Sheets. LENS: AMIENS. September 25th, 1918.

1. 58th Division (Less Artillery) are moving by train 26th inst to AUBIGNY Area.

2. 58th Battalion, M.G.C. will entrain with 173rd Brigade Group at MERICOURT and detrain at ~~LIGNY ST. FLOCHEL.~~ ACQ

3. Battalion H.Q., "A" Company and "B" Company will proceed by train No.5. Time of departure 8.38 p.m.
"C" and "D" Companies will proceed by train No.6. Time of departure 11.38 p.m.

4. Transport will arrive 3 hours and personnel 1½ before the time of departure of trains

5. Supply wagons will be loaded full on trains with units.

6. "A" Company will detail one Officer to act as entraining Officer for No.5 train. "C" Company an Officer for No.6 train. They will report to 173rd Brigade Group entraining Officer at R.T.O's Office. MERICOURT. 3 hours before departure of train.
They will be responsible for the entraining of their respective Groups i.e.,
No 5 train H.Q., "A" and "B" Companies.
No 6 train "C" and "D" Companies.
A loading party of 2/24th London Regiment will be available for both trains.

7. Entraining States will be completed on attached pro formas and handed in to Battalion H.Q. by 6 p.m. to-night 25th inst without fail.
Entraining Officers detailed will report to Battalion H.Q. for full instructions and to collect the entraining states at 7 p.m. to-night 25th inst.

8. "B" and "D" Companies will detail an Officer to act as detraining ~~Officer~~ Officer for their respective train groups.
An unloading party of 2/2nd London Regiment will be available for detraining of both trains.

9. The march to MERICOURT will be carried out as follows:-

H.Q. and "A" Company will fall in at Battalion H.Q. ready to march off at 1 p.m. Route, MAMETZ - MEAULTE - TREUX - MERICOURT.
"C" and "D" Companies will move off under orders of Major W. EMSLIE, O.C. "D" Company 3 hours later by same route.
Transport of H.Q. and "A" Company under Lieut. O.P.PRATT will move by same route at 11.30.a.m.
Transport of "C" and "D" Companies under Lieut. R.C.HALL at 2.30 p.m.

10. All tentage in possession of Companies and H.Q. will be returned direct to Area Commandant MONTAUBAN to-morrow 26th by 10 a.m. Duplicate receipts to be handed in to this Office by 11 a.m.

T.WARNING. Capt & Adjt.

Distribution.

1. "A" Coy. 58th Bn.
2. "B" " do.
3. "C" " do.
4. "D" " do.
5. 58th Division "G".
6. Q.M. and T.O.
7. Signal Officer.
8. O.C. 58th Bn.
9. War Diary.
10. File.

APPENDIX I

SECRET. **58th BATTALION, MACHINE GUN CORPS.** Copy No 13

OPERATION ORDER NO 38.

Ref Sheet 44B 1/40.000. Sept 28th 1918.

1. 58th Division (less Artillery) are relieving the 24th Division on 29th and 30th inst.

2. 58th Battalion M.G.C. will relieve 24th Battalion M.G.C. on 29th inst as follows:-
   "B" Coy 58th Bn (with 174 Bde) will relieve the Coy 24th Bn in LEFT BRIGADE SECTOR.
   "A" Coy 58th Bn (with 173 Bde) will relieve the Coy 24th Bn in CENTRE BRIGADE SECTOR.
   "C" Coy 58th Bn (with 175 Bde) will relieve the Coy 24th Bn in RIGHT BRIGADE SECTOR.
   "D" Coy 58th Bn will relieve the Coy 24th Bn in Divisional Reserve at FOSSE 2.

3. Personnel of Battalion will move by bus from present billets to-morrow 29th inst in accordance with attached Embussing Programme.

4. The whole Battalion Transport will move off under Lt O.P.PRATT, M.C., to-morrow 29th inst at 9.30.a.m. to FOSSE 2, route - BOYEFFLES - FOSSE 10 - Pt. SAINS.

5. Guns, Tripods, Condenser bags and tubes, Spare Parts cases only will be taken.in. The following Stores being taken over at each position for which receipts in duplicate will be sent to Battalion H.Q. by 30th inst:-
   10 Belt boxes, filled.
   10 Belts in improvised boxes.
   S.A.A.
   Reserve Rations (a separate receipt in duplicate).
   Other Stores.

6. All schemes, maps, aeroplane photos and orders relating to the Sector will betaken over.

7. The present arrangements for Harassing Fire will be carried.on.

8. Signal Officer will arrange to take over communications with his opposite number.

9. Relief complete will be reported to Battalion H.Q. and Brigades.

10. Battalion H.Q. will close at GRAND SERVINS at 10.30 a.m. 29th inst and open at FOSSE 2 on arrival.

T.WATKINS, Capt & Adjt.

Distribution.
1. O.C. 58th M.G.Bn.
* 2. O.C. "A" Coy.
* 3. O.C. "B" "
* 4. O.C. "C" "
* 5. O.C."D" "
6. 58th Division "G".
7. 173rd Inf Bde.
8. 174th Inf Bde.
9. 175th " "
10. 24th M.G.Bn.
* 11. Transport Officer.
* 12 Signal Officer.
13. War Diary.
14. File.

* Recipients of Embussing Programme.

58th BATTALION MACHINE GUN CORPS.

EMBUSSING PROGRAMME.

Unit.	No of busses	Time of embussing	Embussing Point.	Debussing Point.	Remarks.
H.Q.	4.	10.30	GOUY SERVINS - PETIT SERVINS ROAD. Head of column facing PETIT SERVINS.	PT. SAINS - BULLY GRENAY ROAD. (Fosse2if possible)	Companies will halt at Fosse 2 for dinner and will then move off for relief meeting Section guides at respective Coy. H.Q.
A.	7.	"	do.	do.	
B.	7.	"	do.	do.	
D.	7.	"	do.	do.	
C.	7.	11.30	Same road but with head of column facing GOUY SERVINS.	SOUCHEZ.	Guns in trench bags, tripods, condenser bags and tubes and spare parts cases will be taken on busses. Meet limbers of 24th Bn at Debussing Point which will carry guns to their Coy.H.Q., where Section guides will be met.

9

58 Division "A".

=====================

Herewith original War Diary of the Battalion under my command, for the period I.10.18 to 31.10.18.

[signature] Lieut Col.

7.11.18 cmdg 58 Battalion M.G.Corps.

Write

Instructions regarding War Diaries and Intelligence Summaries are contained in F. S. Regs., Part II. and the Staff Manual respectively. Title pages will be prepared in manuscript.

WAR DIARY
or
~~INTELLIGENCE SUMMARY.~~
(*Erase heading not required.*)

Army Form C. 2118.

58th Batt.n Machine Gun Corps October 1st – 31st

Place	Date	Hour	Summary of Events and Information	Remarks and references to Appendices
FOSSE 2. L28c	1st		Coys in the line in positions as taken over from the 24th M.G. Battn	
			A Coy in centre sector }	
			B " " left " " } in front of LENS.	44.A.
			C " " Right " " }	
			D Coy in Divisional reserve at Fosse 2	
			Reports were received from the 15th Division that the enemy were retiring on their front. Harassing fire was carried out by A & C Coys in the line	
			2nd Lt F.H. STIRLING & 2nd Lt F. DIXON joined from the Base. Casualties 3. O.R.	
	2nd		Definite news that the enemy was withdrawing to a line PONT à VENDIN – MEURCHIN CANAL. The 15th Div pushed forward to HULLUCH – L.E. without opposition. Instructions were issued to Brigades to push forward strong patrols to ascertain if the enemy had withdrawn on our front. Patrols pushed forward to GREEN LINE which they reported completely captured in the evening. In accordance with instructions the guns of A & B Coys moved forward leaving C Coy	

A5834 Wt W4973/M687 750,000 8/16 D. D. & L. Ltd. Forms/C.2118/13.

Instructions regarding War Diaries and Intelligence Summaries are contained in F. S. Regs., Part II. and the Staff Manual respectively. Title pages will be prepared in manuscript.

WAR DIARY
or
~~INTELLIGENCE SUMMARY.~~
(Erase heading not required.)

Army Form C. 2118.

58th BATTALION.
MACHINE GUN CORPS
Oct 1st – 31st.

Place	Date	Hour	Summary of Events and Information	Remarks and references to Appendices
FOSSE 2.	2nd		in their original positions & now in Divisional Reserve.	~~44~~ A
			D Coy remained at Fosse "2". Enemy reported to be vacating LENS.	
			Casualties 4 OR. 2 OR joined from Base.	
	3rd		D Coy moved from FOSSE 2 to MAROC remaining in Divisional	
			Reserve. Instructions were issued to Brigades to push forward on to	
			the BLUE LINE. Later LENS was reported clear of the enemy and	
			our troops establishing themselves on its eastern outskirts, many	
			explosions occurred in LENS due to mines etc. B & C Coys remained	
			in Divisional Reserve. 4 OR casualties. 2 OR rejoined from Hospital.	
	4th		B Coy HQ moved to QUARRY & A Coy HQ to "CAMERON CASTLE."	M.G.W. N.7.b.c.
			The two guns of C Coy on the GREEN CROSSING (N20c) were withdrawn	
			to M24a 90 80. LIEUT. L.G. DOMINY joined from BASE.	
			2nd Lt. L. CRINE, 2 Lt J. G. N DEWAR, 2nd Lt R.C.R. RICHARDS also joined	
			from Base. 2nd Lt GRAYSON & 6 OR gassed.	
			The BLUE Line now occupied by our troops.	
			Harassing fire carried out by Coys in the line.	

A5834 Wt. W4973/M687 750,000 8/16 D. D. & L. Ltd. Forms/C.2118/13

Instructions regarding War Diaries and Intelligence Summaries are contained in F. S. Regs., Part II. and the Staff Manual respectively. Title pages will be prepared in manuscript.

WAR DIARY

~~or~~

~~INTELLIGENCE SUMMARY.~~

(*Erase heading not required.*)

Army Form C. 2118.

53rd Bn. M.G.C.

October 1st - 31st

Place	Date	Hour	Summary of Events and Information	Remarks and references to Appendices
FOSSE 2.	5		The front was patrolled by the infantry, but the enemy was found to be holding out in strength. The front was quiet by day but much gas shelling by the enemy at night. Harassing fire was carried out by the Coys in the line. C & D Coy remained in Divisional Reserve.	Sheet 44.A.
	6th		Situation quiet no further change on the front enemy still in strength. Harassing fire carried out. C & D Coy remained in Div Reserve.	
	7th		Situation as before Coys in same position. Harassing fire carried out by night.	
	8th		Situation quiet. At night D Coy moved up and relieved A Coy in the right sector, on completion of relief billets were taken over at "MAROC". Harassing fire carried out at night by Coys in the line. C Coy remained in Div Reserve. R.S.M. Cox W.O. joined from Base.	APPENDIX 1.
	9th		Situation quiet dispositions as before. At night C Coy moved forward and relieved B Coy in the ANNAY (left) Sector.	

A5834 Wt. W4973/M687 750,000 8/16 D. D. & L. Ltd. Forms/C.2118/13.

Instructions regarding War Diaries and Intelligence Summaries are contained in F. S. Regs., Part II. and the Staff Manual respectively. Title pages will be prepared in manuscript.

WAR DIARY ~~or~~ ~~INTELLIGENCE SUMMARY.~~

(*Erase heading not required.*)

Army Form C. 2118.

58th Battn M.G.C. October 1st - 31st

Place	Date	Hour	Summary of Events and Information	Remarks and references to Appendices
FOSSE. 2.	9th		On relief B Coy moved to Billets in "ANGRES" (1724233) Harassing fire carried out at night.	
	10th		Situation unchanged C Coy in ANNAY (left) Sector D Coy in HARNES (Right) sector A & B Coy in Div Reserve. Harassing fire carried out at night. 10 OR joined from Base	
	11th		B Coys rear HQ and transport moved forward to ANGRES and joined the adv. HQ. C & D in same positions carried out harassing fire.	
	12th		B Coy moved in the line, taking over from section of 12th MG Bn. D Coy HQ moved to N4d 33. Harassing fire carried out by D Coy. C Coy withdrew from positions at N1b 80. A Coy in reserve at "MAROC"	
MAROC.	13th	11am	Battalion HQ closed at FOSSE 2 and opened at "MAROC" M3. A Coy in Reserve at "MAROC" Carried out training. B Coy HQ situated at O9b 6.3. C Coy marched to billets in O15c. 10.30. D Coy 12 guns in the line. 4 guns in reserve at CHQ N12 39.	[illegible]

A5834 Wt. W4973/M687 750,000 8/16 D. D. & L. Ltd. Forms/C.2118/13.

Instructions regarding War Diaries and Intelligence Summaries are contained in F. S. Regs., Part II. and the Staff Manual respectively. Title pages will be prepared in manuscript.

WAR DIARY
or
~~INTELLIGENCE SUMMARY.~~
(Erase heading not required.)

Army Form C. 2118.

53rd Battalion Machine Gun Corps October 1st – 31st

Place	Date	Hour	Summary of Events and Information	Remarks and references to Appendices
MAROC	14th	-	A Coy remained in reserve at 'MAROC' and carried out training	229 - 42
			B Coy HQ at O9b 6.3.	
			C Coy HQ at 'FOUQUIERES' 1 OR joined from the base	
			D Coy in the line carried out harassing fire 12,000 rounds expended.	
	15th	0700	A Coy moved from 'MAROC' and marched to HARNES being attached to the 173 Inf Bde. Two sect were moved up to CANAL in I28a to bring covering fire to bear on EPINOY & CARVIN but owing to the position of the 15th Div being obscure this was not carried out	APPENDIX 2.
			B Coy HQ moved to O22c7.6.	
			C Coy received orders to relieve all guns of B Coy in the Bde sector.	
			D Coy remained in the line CHQ O8a7.5.	
	16th		'A' Coy and the 173 Bde were withdrawn into Divisional Reserve. the two forward sections being brought back to 'HARNES'	APPENDIX 3
			B Coy HQ moved to 'COURRIERES' (O5a.)	
			C Coy HQ moved to COURRIERES also (I35d) later in the day No 10 & 12 secs were withdrawn to CHQ D Coy in line as before.	
			LIEUT T.B. FRANCES joined from Base	

A5834 Wt. W4973/M687 750,000 8/16 D. D. & L. Ltd. Forms/C.2118/13.

Instructions regarding War Diaries and Intelligence Summaries are contained in F. S. Regs., Part II. and the Staff Manual respectively. Title pages will be prepared in manuscript.

WAR DIARY
~~or~~
~~INTELLIGENCE SUMMARY.~~
(Erase heading not required.)

Army Form C. 2118.

58th Battalion
Machine Gun Corps
October 1st – 31st

Place	Date	Hour	Summary of Events and Information	Remarks and references to Appendices
MONTIGNY O23a2550	16th		Battalion HQ closed at 'MARQ' and opened at 'MONTIGNY'	Sheet 44A 1 pull
			D Coy were withdrawn from the line and concentrated in HARNES under	
			orders of B.G.C. 173 Bde	
	17th		A Coy moved with 173 Inf Bde to 'COURRIERES'	
			B Coy HQ moved to 'OIGNES'	
			C Coy HQ moved to OSTRICOURT	P6a8.8
			D Coy moved in the afternoon to COURRIERES (joining 173 Inf Bde)	O5b2.7
			2nd Lt O.C. Taylor joined from base. Casualties 1 O.R.	
	18.		173 Inf Bde with A & D Coys moved to LE HEM	
			B Coy HQ moved to 'MONS EN PEVELLE'	
			C Coy moved off and were joined by No 9 & 11 sections at LE FOREST	
			HQ + 9 + 11 secs reached RUE COLETTE where they billeted for the night	
	19th		Battalion HQ closed at MONTIGNY (O23) and opened at BERSEE	L21
			A Coy with the 173 Bde continued forward and took up billets in ELOIER	
			Orders issued for 173 Bde to pass through the outpost line on following morning	

A5834 Wt. W4973/M687 750,000 8/16 D. D. & L. Ltd. Forms/C.2118/13.

Instructions regarding War Diaries and Intelligence Summaries are contained in F. S. Regs., Part II. and the Staff Manual respectively. Title pages will be prepared in manuscript.

WAR DIARY
or
~~INTELLIGENCE SUMMARY.~~
(Erase heading not required.)

Army Form C. 2118.

58th Battalion
Machine Gun Corps
Oct 1st - 31st

Place	Date	Hour	Summary of Events and Information	Remarks and references to Appendices
BERSÉE	19th		one section of A Coy being placed in the Advance Guard.	Sheet 44
			B Coy HQ moved to VERT Bois	
			C Coy HQ moved forward with the main body one section with advance Guard. The remaining 3 sections joined CHQ and all proceeded to billets at FERME DU CHAPITRE. Civilians not evacuated from these villages	
			D Coy HQ at LE HEM the Coy put on half an hours notice to move	Appendix 4
	20th		Advance continued by 1730 - one sect A Coy in adv guard remainder of Coy in main body. outpost line established B29 & H5. 2 guns in outpost line & guns in PLANARD. Remainder of Coy & HQ in LANNAY. One section detailed for advance guard on the following day	Sheet 44
		1000	C Coy moved off via NOMAIN to AIX, where they were billeted. One section took up position to cover line of resistance through I3d, I7a, H6.a	Appendix 5.
			D Coy moved from LEHEM to AUCHY arriving at 1100 hrs.	
			B Coy moved to NOMAIN & occupied billets there	

A5834 Wt. W4973/M687 750,000 8/16 D. D. & L. Ltd. Forms/C.2118/13.

Army Form C. 2118.

WAR DIARY
or
~~INTELLIGENCE SUMMARY.~~
(Erase heading not required.)

Instructions regarding War Diaries and Intelligence Summaries are contained in F. S. Regs., Part II. and the Staff Manual respectively. Title pages will be prepared in manuscript.

58th Battalion
Machine Gun Corps
October 1st - 31st

Place	Date	Hour	Summary of Events and Information	Remarks and references to Appendices
PLANARD	21st		Batt HQ closed at BERSEE and opened at PLANARD	Sheet 44 B30.c
			1 Section of A Coy with the 2/24th Londons continued the advance a line being established along the canal through C19 2 25. The remainder of A Coy moved forward to RONGY and then two sections were moved to the FME de MAIRESSE to give covering fire in case of necessity, if the Engineers if they attempted putting down a bridge	C24.c
			B Coy remained at NOMAIN in reserve.	
			C Coy HQ, with 1 section in reserve, established at Chateau [illegible]	
		0900	D Coy moved from AUCHY to RUMEGIES Casualties 3 OR	
	22nd	0400	Attempt made by the 173 Bde to cross the canal assisted by two sections of A Coy also the 2 sects at the FME de MAIRESSE were moved forward to give covering fire	
		0830	Attempt at crossing the canal was abandoned, and the 2 sects were withdrawn to the FME de MAIRESSE. At night these sections carried out harassing fire. B Coy in reserve at NOMAIN carried out training	

A5834 Wt. W4973/M687 750,000 8/16 D. D. & L. Ltd. Forms/C.2118/13.

Army Form C. 2118.

WAR DIARY
or
~~INTELLIGENCE SUMMARY.~~
(Erase heading not required.)

Instructions regarding War Diaries and Intelligence Summaries are contained in F. S. Regs., Part II. and the Staff Manual respectively. Title pages will be prepared in manuscript.

58th Bn
Machine Gun Corps
October 1st - 31st

Place	Date	Hour	Summary of Events and Information	Remarks and references to Appendices
PLANARD.	22nd		C. Coy with 1 sec. at CHQ at Chateau I.4.d	Sheet 44.
			D Coy remained at RUMEGIES but stood by on 15 minutes notice to move.	
			Casualties 1 O.R.	
	23rd		A Coy moved with the 173 Bde HQ to HOWARDRIES. Harassing fire carried out by the guns in the line.	
			B Coy remained at NOMAIN and carried out training.	
			C Coy carried out harassing fire during the night on FORT de MAULDE.	
			D Coy at RUMEGIES carried out training.	
	24th		A Coy in the line with the 173 Bde carried out harassing fire during the night on enemy posts & H.Q.s. 2 O.R. joined from Base	
			B Coy in reserve at NOMAIN	
			C Coys transport moved to RUMEGIES. two sections at CHQ at Chateau I.4.d harassing fire carried out on FORT de MAULDE.	
			D Coy at RUMEGIES in reserve carried out training.	
	25th		A Coy in the line with the 173 Bde Harassing fire carried out during the night	

A5834 Wt. W4973/M687 750,000 8/16 D. D. & L. Ltd. Forms/C.2118/13.

Instructions regarding War Diaries and Intelligence Summaries are contained in F. S. Regs., Part II. and the Staff Manual respectively. Title pages will be prepared in manuscript.

WAR DIARY

~~or~~

~~INTELLIGENCE SUMMARY.~~

(Erase heading not required.)

58th Battalion Machine Gun Corps
58th Bn M G C

Army Form C. 2118.

Place	Date	Hour	Summary of Events and Information	Remarks and references to Appendices
PLANARD	25.		B Coy at NOMAIN in reserve carried out training	Sheet 44
			C Coy in the line, carried out harassing fire in conjunction with	
			a minor operation of the infantry. 3000 rounds were fired on roads etc.	
			D Coy carried out training and were inspected by the Commanding Officer	
			at RUMIGES.	
	26.		One section of D Coy attached to A Coy and one to C Coy.	Appendix 6.
			Harassing fire was carried out by A Coy at night, two guns being	
			used to cover the advance & withdrawal of a patrol.	
			Under orders of the B.G.C. 7th Bde the company started to move up the	
			line, later the move was cancelled and the Coy returned to their billets	
			at NOMAIN. 12 OR reinforcements arrived from Base Depot.	
			C Coy in the line, two sections moved forward to cover [illegible] line.	
			D Coy, two sections remained at RUMIGES and carried out training.	
	27.		A Coy in the line with 173 Bde. in conjunction with the artillery special	
			shoots were carried out on villages in enemy area with success.	
			Constellation being fired on [illegible]	

Instructions regarding War Diaries and Intelligence Summaries are contained in F. S. Regs., Part II. and the Staff Manual respectively. Title pages will be prepared in manuscript.

WAR DIARY
or
~~INTELLIGENCE SUMMARY.~~
(Erase heading not required.)

Army Form C. 2118.

58th Battalion
Machine Gun Corps
October 1st - 31st.

Place	Date	Hour	Summary of Events and Information	Remarks and references to Appendices
PLANARD	27th		B Coy moved under orders of BGC 174 Bde into the line to take over from 173 Bde. C Coy. B Coy HQ at [illegible] Chateau	Sheet 44.
			C Coy on relief by B Coy moved to billets in HAUT HAMMEAU	G10.b
			D Coy less two sections remained at RUMEGIES	
			One sect of D Coy in the line with A Coy moved to I26 2055	
			One sect with OC B Coy moved to I28 8.2	
	28th		A Coy in the line in connection with the Infantry Patrols attempt to cross the canal fire was brought to bear successfully on enemy MGs in D21c and D26b.	
			B Coy in the line. situation unchanged. Transport moved to I13b8.1	
			C Coy in reserve at HAUT HAMMEAU carried out training	
			D Coy less two sects at RUMEGIES carried out training	
	29th		A Coy in the line situation unchanged. harassing fire carried out	
			B Coy No 7 section moved forward with the 7th London Regt and took up position in I9b and I10a.	

A5834 Wt. W4973/M687 750,000 8/16 D. D. & L. Ltd. Forms/C.2118/13

Army Form C. 2118.

Instructions regarding War Diaries and Intelligence Summaries are contained in F. S. Regs., Part II. and the Staff Manual respectively. Title pages will be prepared in manuscript.

WAR DIARY or ~~INTELLIGENCE SUMMARY.~~

(Erase heading not required.)

58th Battalion Machine Gun Corps Oct 1st to 31st

Place	Date	Hour	Summary of Events and Information	Remarks and references to Appendices
PLANARD B30c.	29th		C. Coy at HAUT HAMMEAU carried out training	Sheet 44.
			D Coy (less two sections) at RUMEGIES carried out training.	
	30th		A Coy in the line situation unchanged. Harassing fire was carried out in conjunction with the artillery to cover special infantry patrols of the 3rd London Regt.	
			B Coy in the line carried out harassing fire	
			C Coy at HAUT HAMMEAU carried out training	
			D Coy (less two sections) at RUMEGIES carried out training	
			3 OR casualties	
	31st		A Coy relieved by D Coy and on completion of relief moved to LA VISTERIE in reserve with 173 Bde.	G10 b 35.60
			B Coy in the line situation unchanged carried out harassing fire as usual	
			C Coy in reserve at HAUT HAMMEAU carried out training.	
			D Coy moved up the remaining two sections relieving A Coy	

A5834 Wt. W4973/M687 750,000 8/16 D. D. & L. Ltd. Forms/C.2118/13

Army Form C. 2118.

WAR DIARY

~~or~~

~~INTELLIGENCE SUMMARY.~~

(Erase heading not required.)

Instructions regarding War Diaries and Intelligence Summaries are contained in F. S. Regs., Part II. and the Staff Manual respectively. Title pages will be prepared in manuscript.

58th BATTN.
Machine Gun Corps.
October 1st - 31st

Place	Date	Hour	Summary of Events and Information	Remarks and references to Appendices
PLANARD B30c	31st		D Coy H.Q. moved forward to RONOY CHATEAU (I.4.a) the transport remaining at ROISEL. 2nd Lt F.E. HANCOCK evacuated.	Sheet [illegible]

[illegible] Lieut Col.
Commanding 58th Batt. M.G. Corps.

A5834 Wt. W4973/M687 750,000 8/16 D. D. & L. Ltd. Forms/C.2118/13

APPENDIX 1

SECRET. 58th BATTALION, MACHINE GUN CORPS. Copy No. 11

ORDER No. 32.

Ref Sheets 44A N.W. 1/20,000.
44A S.W. do.

October 7th, 1918.

1. Inter-Company reliefs will take place as follows:-
Night 8/9th, "D" Company will relieve "A" Company in the [illegible] Section. (173rd Infantry Brigade.)
Night 9/10th, "C" Company will relieve "B" Company in the [illegible] Section. (175th Infantry Brigade.)

2. On relief "A" Company will take over billets vacated by "D" Company in [illegible], and will be the Company in Divisional Reserve.
"B" Company will take over, and occupy the Gun positions and Headquarters vacated by "C" Company unless otherwise ordered.

3. All Special Orders, and Information, Maps, Aeroplane photographs, S.O.S. Charts, Harassing Fire Charts, etc., will be handed over.
The Instructions for the Company in Divisional Reserve will be handed over to O.C. "A" Company who will have necessary reconnaissance of BLACK Line carried out as soon as possible after relief.

4. Company Commanders will arrange all details reference Guides etc. Guns and spare parts only should be taken in.

5. Reliefs complete will be reported to Battalion H.Q. and respective Brigades by Code Words:-
For night 8/9th....[illegible]. For night 9/10th....[illegible].

6. Companies to acknowledge.

[illegible], Capt & Adjt.

Distribution.
1. 58th Division "G".
2. 173rd Inf Bde.
3. 174th " "
4. 175th " "
5. O.C. "A" Coy. M.G.Bn.
6. O.C. "B" " "
7. O.C. "C" Coy. M.G.Bn.
8. O.C. "D" " "
9. O.C. 58th M.G.Bn.
10. O.C. Signals, M.G.Bn.
11. War Diary.
12. File.

APPENDIX 2

SECRET. 58th BATTALION, MACHINE GUN CORPS. Copy No. 7...

ORDER No. 40.

1. "A" Company will move from their present location at 0700, 15th inst to HARNES.

2. . They will support 173rd Infantry Brigade in accordance with any order that may be issued.

3. The hour of arrival and exact location to be notified to Battalion H.Qrs. and 173rd Infantry Brigade.

4. "A" Company to acknowledge.

October 14th, 1918.

[signature] Capt & Adjt.

Distribution.
1. 58th Division "G".
2. 173rd Inf Bde.
3. O.C. 58th Bn. M.G.C.
4. O.C. "A" Coy. "
5. O.C. "D" " "
6, O.C. Signals.
7. War Diary.
8. File.

APPENDIX 3.

SECRET. 58th BATTALION, MACHINE GUN CORPS. Copy No. 14

WARNING ORDER.

October 15th, 1918.

Battalion H.Qrs. is probably moving to-morrow 16th inst to MONTIGNY. Exact location and time will be notified later.

Capt & Adjt.,

Distribution.

1. 58th Division "G".
2. 58th Division "A" & "Q".
3. 173rd Inf Bde.
4. 174th " "
5. 175th " "
6. O.C. 58th Bn.MGC.
7. O.C. "A" Coy "
8. O.C. "B" " "
9. O.C. "C" Coy MGC.
10. O.C. "D" " "
11. Transport.Officer.
12. Qr, Mr.
13. O.C. Signals.
14. War Diary.
15. File.

APPENDIX. 4.

[illegible] Battalion [illegible] Orders.

[illegible] Sheet. 44A N.E. 1:20000.
44 [illegible] 1:40000.

To [illegible]

1. [illegible] Company will move at 08.00 hours tomorrow [illegible] 20th inst to [illegible] 14 d.

2. [illegible] will be carried out in tactical formation, i.e. Sections [illegible] with [illegible] at 100 yards intervals.

3. An Officer will be sent forward to billet and will call at Battalion H.Q. en route for any special instructions.

4. [illegible] will be reported to Battalion H.Q.

5. [illegible]

October 19th 1918.

[illegible] Division "G"

T Walkins
Captain and Adjutant
[illegible]

War Diary.

War Diary

APPENDIX. 5.

58th BATTALION MACHINE GUN CORPS.

Sheet 44. Belgium & part of France. 20th October 1918.

1. Battalion H.Q. will move at 0900 hours tomorrow, 21st inst to ~~xxx~~ the Area H.8. Exact location will be notified later.

2. The special Signal Orderly attached to Companies today will bring all messages, reports etc, to a report centre which will be opened at H,15,b.05.95. (Cross Roads). He should not arrive before 1400 hours.

N.B. The destination of B.H.Q. will be subject to alteration dependent on the situation.

[signature]

Capt & Adjt.
58th Bn. M.G.Corps.

[illegible] Bn MGC

File.

APPENDIX. 6.

[illegible]

Acknowledge

[illegible]
[illegible] Bn MGC

Copies to A & C Coys

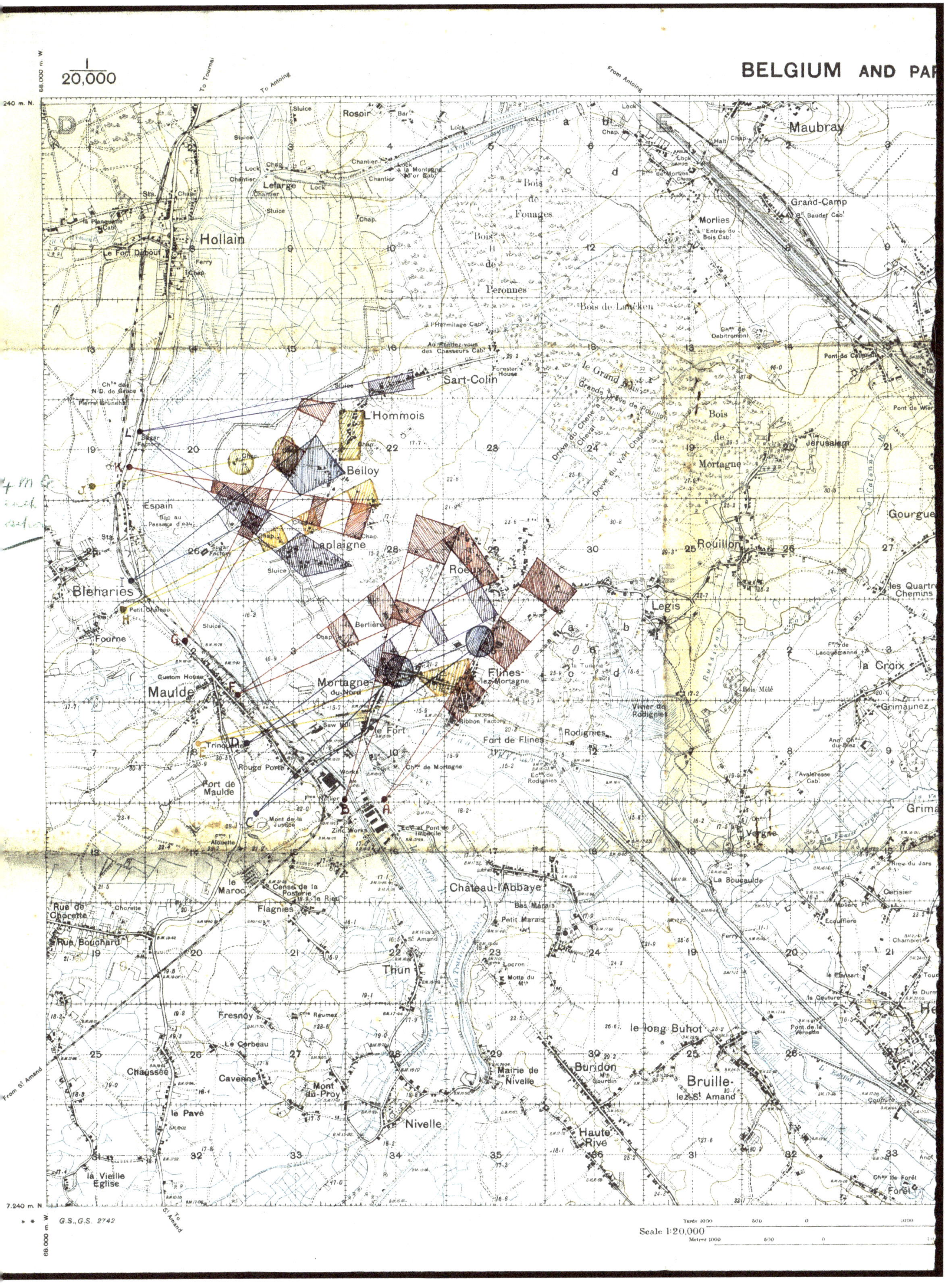

1
20,000

BELGIUM AND PA

To Tournai
To Antoing
From Antoing

D
E

Sluice
Rosoir
Bar
Lock
Chap.
Maubray
Lock
Chantier
Letarge
Chantier
Sluice
Chantier
Lock
la Montagne d'or Cab.
Grand-Camp
Bois de Fouages
Morlies
l'Entrée du Bois Cab.
la Planquette Cab.
Hollain
Le Fort Dubout
Ferry
Bois de Peronnes
Bois de Lanicken
l'Hermitage Cab.
Au Rendez-vous des Chasseurs Cab.
Chau de Debitremont
Pont de Calonne
Chlle de N.D. de Grace
Pierre Brunehaut
Sluice
Sart-Colin
Forester's House
le Grand Bois
Grande Drève de Pouilles
Drève du Chêne à Cheval
Drève du Vert Chasseur
Bois de Mortagne
Jérusalem
Pont de Wiers
L'Hommois
Sugar Factory
Belloy
Espain
Bac au Passage d'eau
Chap.
Laplaigne
Sugar Factory
Sluice
Roeux
Gourgue
Rouillon
Bleharies
Petit Château
les Quatre Chemins
Legis
Fourne
Sluice
Berlière
Chap.
Fme de Lacquemanne
la Croix
Custom House
Maulde
Mortagne-du-Nord
Flines-lez-Mortagne
la Tuilerie
Bois Mêlé
Vivier de Rodignies
Grimaunez
Saw Mill
le Fort
Ribbon Factory
Fort de Flines
Rodignies
Trinq
Rouge Porte
Chau de Mortagne
Ecles de Rodignies
And Cle du Blez
l'Avaleresse Cab.
Port de Maulde
Mont de la Justice
Zinc Works
Ect at Pont de l'Imbecile
Vergne
Grima
Alouette
le Maroc
Cense de la Posterie
le Riez
Château-l'Abbaye
Bas Marais
Petit Marais
Chap.
La Boucaulde
Rieu du Jars
Cerisier
Rue de Chorette
Chorette
Flagnies
Rue Bouchard
St. Amand
Thun
Locron
Motte du Mn
Ferry
Ecouffiere
Champiet
Fresnoy
Fme Reumez
le Corbeau
Chaussée
Caverne
Mont du Proy
Mairie de Nivelle
le long Buhot
Buridon
Mn Gourdin
Bruille-lez-St. Amand
la Couture
Pont de la Vernette
le Pavé
Nivelle
Haute Rive
la Vieille Eglise
Chau de Forêt
Forêt

From St. Amand
To St. Amand

240 m. N.
7.240 m. N.
68,000 m. W.

G.S., G.S. 2742

Scale 1:20,000
Yards 1000 500 0 1000
Metres 1000 500 0

Instructions regarding War Diaries and Intelligence Summaries are contained in F. S. Regs., Part II. and the Staff Manual respectively. Title pages will be prepared in manuscript.

WAR DIARY

~~or~~

~~INTELLIGENCE SUMMARY.~~

(*Erase heading not required.*)

Army Form C. 2118.

58th BATTALION
MACHINE GUN CORPS.
November 1st – 30th 1918.

Vol 8

Place	Date	Hour	Summary of Events and Information	Remarks and references to Appendices
PLANARD. B.30 c	1st		"D" Company and 3 Sections "B" Company in Line. "D" and "B" Companies' H.Q at RONGY CHATEAU – I.4.d.2.7. 1 Section of "B" Company in Reserve in Billets – QUESNOY. Harassing Fire carried out – 27.500 rounds expended. "A" Company in Reserve with 173rd Infantry Brigade at LA VISTERIE, carried out the checking of Gun Stores and cleaning up. "C" Company in Reserve at HAUT HAMEAU carried out Programme of Training.	Sheet 37 ESM
	2nd		Harassing Fire carried out by Companies in Line – 37.500 rounds expended. Reserve Companies carried out usual Training Programme.	ESM
	3rd		"D" Company H.Q. moved to QUESNOY – I.11.a.3.3. Ammunition expended in Harassing Fire 40.150 rounds. The usual Training was carried out by Companies in Reserve.	ESM
	4th		Inter-section Relief carried out by "B" Company. 40.000 rounds were expended in Harassing Fire. "A" Company carried out Training Programme. "C" Company was inspected by G.O.C., 58th Division.	ESM
	5th		Harassing Fire – 40.500 rounds. Reserve Companies carried out Programme of Training.	ESM
	6th		Harassing Fire – 43.500 rounds. Reserve Companies carried out Programme of Training.	ESM
	7th		48.000 rounds were expended in Harassing Fire. 1 Section of "A" Company practised Special Exercise for Tactical Advance Guard.	ESM
			Strength 1st to 7th incl. Decrease – casualties – Officers 2. O.R. 13. Increase – reinforcements – Officers 1. O.R. 30.	

A5834 Wt. W4973/M687 750,000 8/16 D. D. & L. Ltd. Forms/C.2118/13

Army Form C. 2118.

Instructions regarding War Diaries and Intelligence Summaries are contained in F. S. Regs., Part II. and the Staff Manual respectively. Title pages will be prepared in manuscript.

WAR DIARY
or
~~INTELLIGENCE SUMMARY.~~

(Erase heading not required.)

Place	Date	Hour	Summary of Events and Information	Remarks and references to Appendices
PLANARD B.30.c.	8th		Enemy commenced further retirement. "B" Company H.Q and Nos 7 & 8 Sections moved to BLEHARIES Nos 5 & 6 Sections moved under orders of 6th & 8th London Regiments respectively. "D" Company moved to FOURNES - J.1.a.7.4. "A" Company carried out Training Programme. "C" Company H.Q moved to RUE DE QUESNOY - Transport to RUMEGIES.	Sheet 44. FM
BLEHARIES D.19.d.6.4.	9th		Battalion H.Q moved by March Route to BLEHARIES. "A" Company moved with 173rd Brigade to RONGY - I.5.a.4.1. "B" Company (less 5 & 6 Sections) moved to CALLENELLE, Nos 5 & 6 Sections under Command of 6th & 8th London Regiments. No. 10 Section of "C" Company moved off to join Advance Guard. Company moved by March Route to PERUWELZ. "D" Company moved to RŒUX - J.29.c.05.30.	FM
WIERS. E.5.a.05.25	10th		Battalion H.Q moved to WIERS. "A" Coy moved to QUESNOY - I.11.c.6.6. "B" Company (less 2 Sections) moved to BELŒIL. "C" Company, No 11 Section, moved off to join Advance Guard, remainder of Company moved to ECACHERIES. "D" Company at RŒUX.	FM Sheet 44 & 45
BELŒIL. B.3.c.8.3.	11th		Battalion H.Q moved by March Route to BELŒIL.	FM Sheet 45
		1100	Armistice Signed. "A" Company moved to BASECLES - A.14.c.3.1. "B" Company moved to RUE DUBOIS. No 5 Section rejoining Company. No. 12 Section of "C" Company withdrawn to ECACHERIES. "D" Company move to BASECLES.	
	12th		All Companies carried out Training Programmes	FM
	13th		do do do do No 11 Section "C" Company withdrawn to NEUFMAISON.	
	14th		do do do do No 6 Section of "B" Company rejoined Company	
			Strength - 8th to 14th incl. Decrease - casualties 31 Other Ranks.	

A5834 Wt. W4973/M687 750,000 8/16 D. D. & L. Ltd. Forms/C.2118/13

Army Form C. 2118.

Instructions regarding War Diaries and Intelligence Summaries are contained in F. S. Regs., Part II. and the Staff Manual respectively. Title pages will be prepared in manuscript.

WAR DIARY
or
~~INTELLIGENCE SUMMARY.~~

(Erase heading not required.)

Place	Date	Hour	Summary of Events and Information	Remarks and references to Appendices
BELOEIL. B.3.c.8.3.	15th		Training Programmes carried out. Thanksgiving Services for all denominations.	Sheet 45.
	16th		do do do.	
	17th		Church Parades.	E.G.M.
	18th		Training Programmes carried out. No 9 Section, "C" Company rejoined Company. Prepare to move to New Area.	
ROUCOURT. F.14.d.70.25	19th		"A" Company with Transport inspected by B.G.C, 173rd Brigade. Battalion concentrated in ROUCOURT Area. H.Q., "A" & "D" Companies in ROUCOURT. "B" & "C" Companies in BURY.	Sheet 44 E.G.M.
	20th & 21st		Training and Educational Schemes carried out. Lieut Col. C.J. WILEY, D.S.O., to U.K. 21/11/18. Lieut Col E.G. MERCER, C.M.G, joined and took over Command of Bn. 21/11/18. Strength 15th to 21st incl. Decrease - casualties - Officers 2. O.R 15. Increase - reinforcements - Officers 1. O.R. 5.	E.G.M.
	22nd & 23rd		Training and Educational Schemes carried out.	
	24th		Church Parades.	
	25th - 30th		Training and Educational Schemes carried out. 26th "A" & "D" Companies inspected by C.O. 27th "B" & "C" do do do. Strength 22nd to 30th incl. Decrease - casualties - O.R 13. Increase reinforcements. Officers 1. O.R. 49.	E.G.M.

E.G. Mercer Lieut. Col.
Cmdg. 58 Battn. M.G. Corps

A5834 Wt. W4973/M687 750,000 8/16 D. D. & L. Ltd. Forms/C.2118/13

58th BATTALION MACHINE GUN CORPS.

SECRET.

7th November 1918.

Instructions for forthcoming operations.

MACHINE GUNS.

1. For the crossing of the River and Canal the 58th M.G.Bn. will be employed as follows:-

Attached to 174th Brigade., "B" Coy. less 2 Sections.
Attached to 175th Brigade., "C" Coy. less 2 Sections.

"A" Coy. with 2 Sections of "B" Coy. attached, and "D" Coy. with 2 Sections of "C" Coy attached, will support the crossing and subsequent advance by a covering barrage under orders of O.C. Bn.

2. The 2 Sections of "B" & "C" Coys employed on barrage fire will on the completion of their task revert to their respective Coy. Commanders.

3. The machine guns will be employed in Batteries of 4 guns each, and these batteries will be lettered from A to L. Batteries A to F will be grouped under the command of O.C. "A" Company and will cover the front of 174th Brigade. Batteries G to L will be grouped under the command of O.C. "D" Company and will cover the front of 175th Brigade.

4. The Battery positions and the targets for each, are shown on the attached map. Each Battery Commander will have a chart showing the exact times for lifts etc.
Except C.E. & I. all Batteries are given 3 distinct targets.

5. At Zero all Batteries will open fire on the near edge of their first targets and at Zero plus - mins, will elevate gradually so as to reach the farther edge of that target at Zero plus - mins, when they will lift unto their 2nd target. Fire will be maintained on their 2nd targets until Zero plus - mins and then lift unto their 3rd targets on which fire will be maintained until Zero plus - mins.

6. The rate of fire will be on 1st targets, 100 rounds a minute, on 2nd targets 50 rounds a minute and on 3rd targets, 75 rounds a minute.

7. If visibility allows and where direct fire can be obtained, a special look out will be posted to watch for enemy M.Gs. which will be immediately engaged.

8. Prior to Zero the usual harassing fire will be maintained.

A. P. Wiley
Lieut. Col.
Commanding, 58th Battalion M.G.Corps.

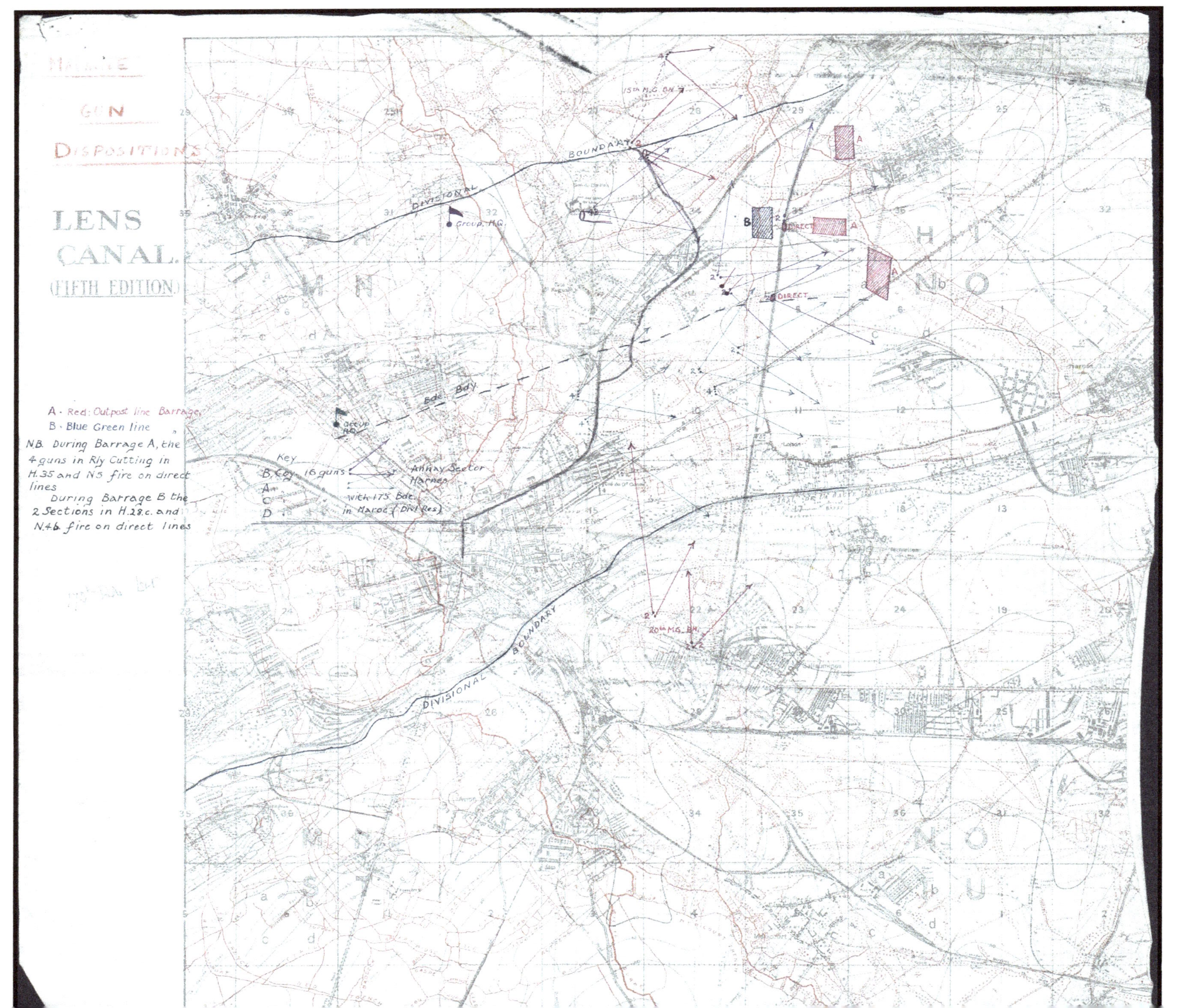
GUN
DISPOSITIONS
LENS
CANAL.
(FIFTH EDITION)
A · Red: Outpost line Barrage
B · Blue Green line "
N.B. During Barrage A, the 4 guns in Rly Cutting in H.35 and N5 fire on direct lines
During Barrage B the 2 Sections in H.28.c. and N.4b. fire on direct lines
Key
B Coy 16 guns
A
C
D
Anway Sector Harnes
with 175 Bde in Maroc (Divl Res)
Group H.Q.
Bde Bdy
DIVISIONAL BOUNDARY
15th M.G. BN
20th M.G. BN
DIRECT
A
B

Instructions regarding War Diaries and Intelligence Summaries are contained in F. S. Regs., Part II. and the Staff Manual respectively. Title pages will be prepared in manuscript.

WAR DIARY

~~or~~

~~INTELLIGENCE SUMMARY.~~

(*Erase heading not required.*)

Army Form C. 2118.

58th BATTALION, MACHINE GUN CORPS.

December 1st - 31st 1918

Place	Date	Hour	Summary of Events and Information	Remarks and references to Appendices
ROUCOURT. F.14.d.70.25.	1st.	-	Battalion inspected by Commanding Officer. Educational Training carried out. E.S.M.	Map Sheet 44.
	2nd	L	Battalion march to GRANDGLISE. Inspection of the whole Division by General Sir H.S. HORNE K.C.B., K.C.M.G., Commanding First Army.	
	3rd - 7th		Training, Educational Programmes and Route Marches carried out. E.S.M.	
	8th		Church Parades.	
	9th - 14th		Training, Educational Programmes, and Route Marches carried out. E.S.M.	
	15th		Church Parades	
	16th - 21st		Training, Educational Programmes, and Route Marches carried out. E.S.M.	
	22nd		Church Parades.	
	23rd - 28th		Training, Educational Programmes, and Route Marches carried out. E.S.M.	
	29th		Church Parades.	
	30th - 31st		Training, Educational Programmes, and Route Marches carried out. E.S.M. Strength for month – Increases – Officers Nil Other Ranks 19. Decreases – Officers 1 Other Ranks 66.	

E.S. Mercer Lieut Colonel
Commanding 58th Bn M. G. Corps

A5834 Wt. W4973/M687 750,000 8/16 D. D. & L. Ltd. Forms/C.2118/13.

4

Instructions regarding War Diaries and Intelligence Summaries are contained in F. S. Regs., Part II. and the Staff Manual respectively. Title pages will be prepared in manuscript.

WAR DIARY

or

~~INTELLIGENCE SUMMARY.~~

(*Erase heading not required.*)

Army Form C. 2118.

58th Battalion Machine Gun Corps. January 1st to 31st 1919

Place	Date	Hour	Summary of Events and Information	Remarks and references to Appendices
Roncourt. F14 d 72.	1st to 4th		Training, educational programmes & route marches carried out.	
	5th		Church Parades.	
	6th to 11th		Training, educational programmes & route marches carried out.	
	12th		Church Parades.	
	13th to 18th		Training, educational programmes & route marches carried out.	
	19th		Church Parades.	
	20th to 25th		Training, educational programmes & route marches carried out.	
	26th		Church Parades.	
	27th to 31st		Training, educational programmes & route marches carried out.	

Strength for whole month:- Increase officers 1. O.R. 13.
Decrease officers 6. O.R. 238.
(Demobilization).

E.S. Mence
Lieut. Colonel
Commanding 58th Battalion Machine Gun Corps.

A5834 Wt. W4973/M687 750,000 8/16 D. D. & L. Ltd. Forms/C.2118/13.

3/3

S E C R E T.
=*=*=*=*=*=*=*=*=*=

58th Division "A".

Herewith Original. War Diary for the month of February for the Battalion under my Command.

I Watkins Capt & Adjt.

for Major,

March 1st, 1919. Commanding 58th Battalion, Machine Gun Corps.

58

Army Form C. 2118.

Instructions regarding War Diaries and Intelligence Summaries are contained in F. S. Regs., Part II. and the Staff Manual respectively. Title pages will be prepared in manuscript.

WAR DIARY or INTELLIGENCE SUMMARY.

(Erase heading not required.)

58th Battalion, Machine Gun Corps

1st to 28th February, 1919

Place	Date	Hour	Summary of Events and Information	Remarks and references to Appendices
ROUCOURT	Feb. 1st.		Training, Educational Programmes and Route Marches carried out.	Sheet 44
	2nd.		Church Parades	
	3rd-8th		Training, Educational Programmes and Route Marches carried out.	
	9th		Church Parades	
	10th-15th		Training, Educational Programmes and Route Marches carried out.	
	16th		Church Parades	
	17th-22nd		Training, Educational Programmes and Route Marches carried out.	
	23rd.		Church Parades.	
LEUZE	24th		Battalion move by march route to LEUZE.	Sheet 37
	25th-28th		Training, Educational Programmes and Route Marches carried out.	R35 b.2.9.

Strength for whole month

	Off.	O.R.
Increase	–	1
Decrease	4	193

D. Ralston Major.
Cmdg. 58th Batt. M.G.C.

A5834 Wt. W4973/M687 750,000 8/16 D. D. & L. Ltd. Forms/C.2118/13.

5

Army Form C. 2118.

Instructions regarding War Diaries and Intelligence Summaries are contained in F. S. Regs., Part II. and the Staff Manual respectively. Title pages will be prepared in manuscript.

WAR DIARY
or
INTELLIGENCE SUMMARY.
(Erase heading not required.)

58th Battalion Machine Gun Corps

1st to 31st March 1919

Vol 13

Place	Date	Hour	Summary of Events and Information	Remarks and references to Appendices
LEUZE (Belgium)	1st		Checking and cleaning of Mobilization Equipment	E.S.M.
	2nd		Church parades	
	3-8th		Checking and cleaning of Mobilization Equipment	
	9th		Church parades	
	10-15th		Checking and cleaning of Mobilization Equipment	
	16th		Church parades	
	17-22nd		Checking and cleaning of Mobilization Equipment	
	23rd		Church parades	
	24-29th		Checking and cleaning of Mobilization Equipment	
	30th		Church parades	
	31st		Checking and cleaning of Mobilization Equipment	
			Strength for whole month Increase Officers – O.R.s 2	
			Decrease Officers 22 O.R.s 156	

E.S. Mercer
Commanding 58th Bn. M.G.C.

A5834 Wt. W4973/M687 750,000 8/16 D. D. & L. Ltd. Forms/C.2118/13.

H. Qrs.
58th Div. Group.

Herewith ORIGINAL War Diary for the Battalion under my Command for the month of APRIL, 1919.

8

Captain,

April 30th, 1919. Commanding 58th Battalion, M.G.Corps.

Army Form C. 2118.

58

WAR DIARY
or
INTELLIGENCE SUMMARY.

(*Erase heading not required.*)

Instructions regarding War Diaries and Intelligence Summaries are contained in F. S. Regs., Part II. and the Staff Manual respectively. Title pages will be prepared in manuscript.

April 1st to 30th 1919 — 58th Batt M. G. Corps

Vol 14

Place	Date	Hour	Summary of Events and Information	Remarks and references to Appendices
Leuze (Belgium)	1-5		Checking & cleaning of Mobilization Equipment	L.J.D.
	6		Church parades	
	7-12		Checking & cleaning of Mobilization Equipment	L.J.D.
	13		Church parades	
	14-19		Checking & cleaning of Mobilization Equipment	L.J.D.
	20		Church parades	L.J.D.
	21-26		Checking & cleaning of Mobilization Equipment	
	27		Church parades	L.J.D.
	28-30		Checking & cleaning of Mobilization Equipment	
			Strength for whole month: Increase Officers NIL O.Rs NIL; Decrease Officers 13 O.Rs 149	

L. J. Downing
Captain
Commanding 58th Bn. M. G. Corps

A5834 Wt. W4973/M687 750,000 8/16 D. D. & L. Ltd. Forms/C.2118/13.

54

Army Form C. 2118.

Instructions regarding War Diaries and Intelligence Summaries are contained in F. S. Regs., Part II. and the Staff Manual respectively. Title pages will be prepared in manuscript.

WAR DIARY
or
INTELLIGENCE SUMMARY.

(*Erase heading not required.*)

58th Batt M. G. Corps.
May 1st to 31st 1919

Place	Date	Hour	Summary of Events and Information	Remarks and references to Appendices
LEUZE (Belgium)	1-3		Checking and cleaning of Mobilization Equipment	L.D.
	4		Church Parades.	
	5-10		Checking and cleaning of Mobilization Equipment.	
	11		Church Parades.	
	12-17		Checking and Cleaning of Mobilization Equipment	
	18		Church parades.	
	19-24		Checking and cleaning of Mobilization Equipment	
	25		Church parades.	
	26-31		Checking and cleaning of Mobilization Equipment.	

Strength: Increase Offs — O.R. 9; Decrease 1. 19

L. J. Downes Capt
Commanding 58th Bn M.G.C.

A5834 Wt. W4973/M687 750,000 8/16 D. D. & L. Ltd. Forms/C.2118/13.

www.ingramcontent.com/pod-product-compliance
Lightning Source LLC
Chambersburg PA
CBHW081422160426
43193CB00013B/2171
* 9 7 8 1 4 7 4 5 3 1 1 3 9 *